28—

D1187568

THE CHAPEL HILL SERIES OF NEGRO BIOGRAPHIES

Edited by BENJAMIN BRAWLEY

*

SOJOURNER TRUTH

*

The University of North Carolina Press, Chapel Hill, N. C.;
The Baker and Taylor Company, New York; Oxford University
Press, London; Maruzen-Kabushiki-Kaisha, Tokyo; Edward Evans
& Sons, Ltd., Shanghai; D. B. Centen's Wetenschappelijke Boek-
handel, Amsterdam.

SOJOURNER TRUTH

Sojourner Truth

GOD'S
FAITHFUL
PILGRIM

*

ARTHUR HUFF FAUSET

Author of FOR FREEDOM

*

Chapel Hill
THE UNIVERSITY
of North Carolina
PRESS

PRINTED IN THE UNITED STATES OF AMERICA

Van Rees Press, New York

TO MY MOTHER

Foreword

SOJOURNER TRUTH was a restless shadow—we are tempted to call her God's Shadow, for she constantly haunted her Almighty, never giving him peace until she was satisfied that what she considered to be necessary had been fulfilled. She flitted about the country, here, there, everywhere, so rapidly, so feverishly, that it is difficult to catch more than a flying view of her ever-moving form. These pages, then, are only glimpses of the shadow that was Sojourner Truth: may we catch some of the substance of her restless life! For she is, without doubt, one of America's most spectacular and lovable characters.

Sojourner Truth never learned to read or write. Her speech was couched in the language of the illiterate; we have only glimpses, however, even of this. There appear to be no actual records of her speech taken in her youth or early womanhood, and no attempt has been made in the present volume to invent a dialect for her in this period of her life. Later, however, as people began to quote her or write about her, they tried to reproduce her actual speech, or to represent her as speaking the conventional literary dialect of her race. Therefore, when in the following pages quotations are made from these later sources, it may seem that her English was normal at the beginning of her life and degenerated as she grew older.

This, of course, is not the case. In her childhood she spoke a Dutch jargon, which, even if we knew the language, we probably could not transcribe. Only scattered fragments remain of her early English utterances. Therefore, from her early life as we know it, we are compelled to piece together numerous bits of circumstantial evidence of thinking and speaking, and to consider ourselves fortunate that more complete and accurate records from her later life are extant.

We shall try to keep ever faithful to the facts; yet if, in piecing together certain separate but apparently related items which have come down to us, at times it appears that we may have taken too much for granted in order to achieve a unified and, at the same time, a properly colored picture, let allowance be made for the scant data which exist and for the will-o'-the-wisp nature of the central character.

Of this much we can be certain: Sojourner Truth would be found to-day in the most advanced camp. With Fred Douglass she enjoys the undoubted distinction of being a rebel by nature. Her ideas and her agitational methods frequently align her with the revolutionaries, and this despite her firm allegiance to Jehovah—or shall we say because of it?

We have received an immense amount of help from various sources. Grateful acknowledgment is due Dr. Benjamin G. Brawley, Washington, D. C.; Leon Gardiner, Philadelphia; Dr. John Harvey Kellogg, Battle Creek, Michigan; Dr. Alain Locke, Washington, D. C.; Arthur A. Schomburg, New York City; Henry P. Slaughter, Washington, D. C.; James H. Young and Allan R. Freelon, Philadelphia; and, most of all, Forest H. Sweet, Battle Creek, Michigan, for assistance in obtaining invaluable source material relative to this remarkable person, and for supplying the photographic likeness.

Philadelphia   ARTHUR HUFF FAUSET
February, 1938

Contents

SOJOURNER TRUTH

I

Isabella

IN 1652, AFTER some debate, the Dutch finally voted to permit African slaves to be imported into New Amsterdam.

Not long after, the Negroes in small numbers began to trickle into the colony. By 1720 there were four thousand of these out of a total population of thirty-one thousand. While many had come by way of the West Indies, a large number arrived direct from Africa.

They brought trouble with them. The arrogant colonists would never take kindly to the black fellows who seemed to be a phenomenon of some other world. Nor did the Negroes accept too warmly their new lords. From time to time rumors of organized insurrection stirred the colony, though until considerably later the slaves as a group probably seldom dreamed of anything so elaborate. However, any suspected activity was sufficient cause for arrest and trial—and conviction, sometimes with the death penalty attached.

By the year 1741, when mysterious fires destroyed a few houses scattered here and there in the colony, the settlers became so panicky that they seized upon many of the Negroes, most of them quite innocent, burned thirteen of them at the stake, hanged eighteen, and transferred seventy to other regions. Slavery seemed destined to take as bloody a course in New York as it was later to take along the Mississippi.

It must have been a few years later that a tall black fellow whom the Dutch called Baumfree, "the-straight-

as-a-tree-fellow," received passage from the Gold Coast
via an African trader. He may have had an inkling of his
future, but the chances are that he had fewer ideas on the
subject than most of those European immigrants who
swarmed to America prior to the World War.

Just what part of Africa had been his home, in what
year he was born, or on what date he arrived in the New
World, and precisely where he was taken or what he did
immediately after his arrival, no one to-day knows. It is
a certainty that eventually he reached the colony of New
York, and that he married on three occasions, although,
as far as we know, none of his wives had died, and there
had been no divorce.

Perhaps we do injustice to the term "married," for
courts of law in our time would hardly recognize many
of those old slave marriages. However, it was not at Baumfree's request that each of his first two wives had been
sold away from him. What had a slave to do with these
arrangements? It was the masters who separated slave
wives and husbands, and it was they who afterwards encouraged their robust males to remarry. Had not the good
Lord admonished his children, "Be fruitful and multiply"?
Reason enough for masters to condone a conjugal relationship which probably would prove as tragic in its outcome as it was vicious in its conception.

Baumfree's third and last wife must have been a very interesting and perhaps unique person. It is to her more than
likely that we owe many of the pronounced characteristics of the daughter who is to be the important figure in
this narrative. Doubtless she was as meek and subservient
and tractable as Baumfree appears to have been, but in
addition she had a mind of her own.

Apparently she possessed the inevitable optimism of her
race, was a perpetual moralist, believed that the God of
the slave and the God of the master were one and the same

—and that He was good—and, finally, she was endowed with an unusual intuitive sense. From her the daughter to whom we have referred will inherit a religious zeal bordering on fanaticism, an extraordinary piety, a sense of deep devotion, and an uncanny prescience. Because of this inheritance, her journey through life will be marked with zealousness, a sublime courage, unusual experiences—and achievements far beyond anything her formal development would lead anyone to expect.

The name of this third wife of Baumfree was Elizabeth, but it seems hardly likely that she was ever called anything but a familiar "Mau-Mau-Bett." By the time we make her acquaintance, she has become the mother of a family of ten or twelve boys and girls, all but two of whom have been sold away to other plantations.

Peter, age three years, of whom description is lacking, and Isabella, a spindly, angular-boned, broad-faced, misty-eyed but imperious creature of five, still remain. Whenever Mau-Mau-Bett looks at these two reminders of those others who have been taken from her, a dreadful horror convulses her body and soul. When will these be gone also! Alas! what will there be to look forward to in that day when Nature's course has run, and children come no more?

After Colonel Hardenbergh, Baumfree's owner whom the slaves mistakenly called Ardinburgh, had died, his son Charles erected a new home, outfitting it as a public inn, and providing it with a cellar for slave quarters. This cellar was as dismal as the word indicates. To begin with, there was practically no light. A pane or two of glass just above the ground did let in a few rays of the sun, but these had first to strike the earth outside the house, then be reflected into the glass above, and through it to the floor below.

That word *floor* was a misnomer. A few loose boards covered the uneven earth at the bottom of the cellar, and as often as not water and mud oozed between these, pro-

viding that creepy sensation which one experiences in
going over loose planking that is stretched across a brook.
Still the shivers which coursed up and down the slaves'
spines as they made their treacherous way over these
boards must have been far less distressing than the chills
and the miasma from the damp, noxious fumes of the
cellar. Good health and long life would hardly be vouch-
safed to people dwelling, all sizes, ages, and sexes, in such
a place. Yet here the "bountiful" Marse Charles had established his human chattel. Here on a pallet of straw or
upon filthy old blankets they might squat or sleep. Here,
too, they could inherit a legacy of rheumatism, fever sores,
palsy, and a crippled old age.

One wonders how human beings could laugh or smile
in the midst of these terrible conditions; but the wonder
would be greater if they could live without laughing and
smiling. Life did have its share of fun for these unfortunate
creatures, though it reserved for them a greater measure
of hardship and sorrow. Mau-Mau-Bett and Baumfree
hardly knew whether to feel glad or sorry as they sat
around blazing pine knots for hours in the night, recount-
ing the numerous dramatic incidents which they had witnessed or had been a part of, and which resurrected
themselves in the dim darkness of their cellar retreat.

There was the tragedy of the slave infant who knew no
better than to whimper and cry, to the great annoyance of
the family of its master. For this, one day the master lifted
it in his hands and dashed out its brains against a wall. The
child's grief-stricken mother rushed in for the corpse.
While she was washing the body preparatory for burial,
an Indian passed by. When he inquired what had happened
and had been apprised, he said, "Had I been there then, I
would have put my tomahawk in the murderer's head."

Perhaps so. Indians notoriously were more rebellious
than Negroes. Still the child might have suffered a worse

fate. What about Hasbrouck's slave child? At the age of
five years it could neither talk nor walk. Even its cries were
different from those of normal children, and all it could
do was to keep up a constant moaning sound. Instead of
providing special attention for this subnormal child, Hasbrouck's anger was aroused and he kicked it about as if it
had been a football. He thought nothing of giving the
helpless creature a blow with his foot which would send it
rolling clear across the room. How much better for this
child if it might have died!

The night was filled with stories. The pine logs, crack-
ling and sputtering in the thick gloom of the cellar, lent an
incredible air of cheeriness to the dismal place. Occasionally there was nothing but silence until Baumfree arose to
rake the dying embers. Occasionally, too, low sobbing
cries issued from one of the darkened corners of the cellar
where Mau-Mau-Bett sat huddled and suddenly recalled
an especially tragic moment in her own life.

Tiny Isabella, frightened like all little children clean out
of her wits, cries out disconsolately in the Dutch brogue
which is the only language these slaves know, "Mau-Mau,
why do you groan so?"

The answer is always substantially the same; only details in the language vary.

"Oh, my child," Mau-Mau sobs in a broken jargon
which it is impossible to transcribe, "I am thinking of
your brothers and sisters who have been sold away from
me.

"Michel," she groans, "dear little Michel. . . . How we
loved him. Just your age, daughter . . . . and cunning as a
kitten. . . . . So full of fun!

"One day, he got up early with the birds. It was cold;
snow was on the ground. . . . . See the fire there? . . . . .
Little Michel, small as he was, made a little fire like that
one, only smaller. Then he came rushing to me, calling out,

'Mau-Mau, oh, Mau-Mau...come...come...everything is ready.'"

A flaming-red coal sputters. Mau-Mau speaks slowly and more low.

"And here's your mother and father just a-trembling and crying because we know the horrible man is coming any minute to take him away.....Poor lamb.....He didn't have any idea of what was going to happen.....He couldn't know. How could he? He thought everything would stay just like it was.....always.

"And so, when some bells began to tinkle outside, and a horse and sleigh stopped right outside our door, what must he do but rush straight out of the house and into the sleigh before we could catch hold of him! Oh, he thought it was all great fun—those first few minutes. Then suddenly he stood stock still. He saw something, and he knew that it was very strange."

A deep pause. More hushed tones.

"They were taking his little sister, Nancy, and shutting her up in the sleigh box.....And then he understood! Oh! Oh! Slave snatchers! That's what they were. Slave traders of the master. And they were after Michel, too.

"What a terrible screaming time he had! How he did leap down from the sleigh! Fast. Fast. So fast they couldn't catch him. Into the house he ran. He thought he would be safe if only he got inside the house. Way under the bed he hid himself." (Mau-Mau probably forgot that there were no real beds under which he could hide!)

"And your papa and mother right there beside him, whimpering and crying; but it was no use. They came and got him in no time. Carried him right back to the sleigh. That's the last we saw of him.....The last we ever saw of your brother Michel, or your sister Nancy."

Mau-Mau sobs bitterly. Isabella grasps her arm, shivers, nestles close to her. Tears are in all eyes.

"When will they come and take you, too?"

The question clutches at Mau-Mau's breast.

Sometimes when the weather was clear and the air not too chilly they would all sit outside under the stars and the moon, and Mau-Mau would instruct her two little ones.

"My children," she began, "there is a God who hears and sees everything you think and do."

"A God, Mau-Mau?" the children exclaim—while Isabella with her big dreamy eyes scans her mother's face, then the endless darkness and finally the heavens in her effort to discern the great mystery—"where does He live?"

"He's up there," says Mau-Mau, pointing skyward.

The children are all eyes towards the stars.

"When you are beaten or cruelly treated, and want your master or your mistress to change and become kind to you, or whenever you fall into any kind of trouble, you must ask His help. He will always hear you and help you."

She teaches them the Bible stories, being especially careful to draw their attention to the morals of the stories, which slave masters, of course, had found very appropriate for slave minds.

"Thou must not lie."

"Thou must not steal."

"Servant, obey your master in the Lord."

In a patois which would have been intelligible to a citizen of Amsterdam, mother and children repeated the Lord's prayer.

"Our Father which art in heaven . . . . . Thy will be done . . . . . Give us . . . . our daily bread . . . . and forgive us as we forgive those who trespass against us . . . . . Lead us not into temptation . . . . . Deliver us from evil . . . . forever and ever . . . . .'

Despite her unquestioning faith in God, when Charles Hardenbergh died Mau-Mau-Bett's heart was filled with misgivings. Isabella was about nine years of age, her brother seven. They would bring a nice penny in the auction which was sure to follow in order to clear up the estate. Would they, too, be torn from her as all those other children had been?

They were sitting out under the stars. Suddenly Mau-Mau heaved a deep, bitter groan, and cried out, "Oh, Lord, how long, how long?"

Her children, terrified, called out to her, "What is the matter, Mau-Mau?"

"Oh, matter enough," the baffled mother sobbed. Her eyes were filled with tears, and her heart was broken. "Do you see those stars?" she murmured. "Those same stars and that moon are looking down upon your brothers and sisters. They don't know where I am, and I don't know where they are. Maybe at this very moment they are looking up at this same sky, wherever they be."

Another stifled groan brings grief into her children's hearts. She is unable to express her sorrow in words. All the comfort she has now is this thought that however far away from her or from each other her children may be, at least a communion is possible through the stars. Small enough comfort for a woman who has borne twelve children.

The Hardenberghs had their worries also. An auction of slaves ought to mean profit; but how was profit to be made from useless material? Now there was Baumfree. Already his years were telling on him to a dreadful degree. His limbs had become gnarled and twisted from the constant exposure in damp cellars and unprotected cabins. His bones creaked and ached from rheumatism. His eyes, too, were giving him concern, and he feared blindness. He was an old man far beyond his actual years, an old slave—something less than a man—for a decrepit slave ceased to be a valuable possession, and became, instead, a care and a bother.

"Who is going to be burdened with old Baumfree when we have sold off his faithful Mau-Mau-Bett?" was the question in the calculating minds of the Hardenbergh heirs.

One way to find out was to inquire openly; and this they did. They soon discovered that no one desired the once "straight-as-a-tree-fellow."

Here, then, was a concern. It was one thing to separate able-bodied man and wife; but even the most calloused slave driver would have some qualms about dividing an aged couple who had been together so many years, especially when one was nearly halt and blind. The Hardenberghs finally decided that the money which Mau-Mau-Bett would bring on the auction block was not commensurate with the hardship it would entail for Baumfree; in fact, that they stood to lose rather than profit, since they would have to assume responsibility for Baumfree.

"You take care of your husband, Mau-Mau-Bett," they told Baumfree's wife, "and we will grant you both your freedom."

To slaves such as they, this seemed the greatest boon. Were not many Negroes saving money, hundreds of dollars in fact, in order to purchase just that? Think of the slaves who had died in plots and minor rebellions in the name of that word! Freedom! Quite naturally Baumfree and Mau-Mau-Bett would rejoice at this opportunity to cast off their bonds and spend the remainder of their lives in freedom together. It even assuaged their grief, to some extent, at having to be separated from Isabella and Peter. And to mitigate their sorrow still further, they had the promise of permission to remain in the cellar which had been so long their home. This was real luck. All of it was. At least so they thought.

So they had the slave auction.

This must have been about the year 1806 when Isabella was about nine years old. For despite many assertions to the contrary, every substantial piece of evidence points to Isabella's having been born about 1797. This is an important matter, especially in Isabella's later life, when the question of her age more than once is a consideration. We will digress a moment in order to present the apparent facts.

If we assume that Isabella was born about 1797, it is easy to establish the time of this auction, since she herself has told us that she was about nine years of age at the time. But as the years roll on, Isabella becomes a questionable witness where her age is involved. If we are to take her word for it many years later, we shall have to grant an additional twenty or twenty-five years to her span of life.

We do have the following positive pieces of evidence. In 1835, a person who saw much of her and who wrote a book largely on her account, in which she is a very prominent figure, judged her to be about thirty-eight years of age. If that be true, then Isabella must have been born about 1797. But there is additional evidence. In 1834, Isabella found it desirable to possess a letter of reference from a former master, John Dumont, with whom she had lived nearly twenty years. Dumont states that Isabella came to him in 1810 when she was about twelve or fourteen years of age. In other words, she was about nine years of age in 1806, and was born about 1797.

It is hardly likely that a man would underestimate the age of an adult woman by twenty or more years, which would have to be the case if we are to take Isabella's word many years later rather than the opinion of the person who judged her to be thirty-eight years of age in 1835. But surely Dumont, in 1810, would not have imagined Isabella to be twelve or fourteen years old if she had been thirty or thirty-five at the time.

There will be many persons who, seeing Isabella in later life, will add years, even a quarter century, to her age. We shall be suspicious of all such statements and, until better evidence is adduced, believe that she was born about 1797.

One morning, then, in 1806, a crowd of people came to the Hardenbergh estate, probably dressed quite fashionably, the men in high hats and cutaway coats, the ladies in the latest modes from Paris (or they may all have been quite an inelegant, nondescript crowd), and listened to the auctioneer who with his hammer struck off bargains in human flesh to the familiar sound of "Going, going, gone."

It did not take long for Isabella to go, for John Nealy of Ulster County, New York, received her for the paltry sum of one hundred dollars—no price at all for a slave. There is some rumor that a few sheep were thrown into the bargain!

Could a certain lack of feminine charm have been the reason for such a low figure? But then slaves were not purchased for their beauty. Could it have been a saucy cock of the head, and an imperious thrust of the body as she walked, or even, perhaps, a suggestion of incompetence due to those mist-blown eyes of hers which seemed always to be far away as if longing for something they did not possess, and the stupid Dutch jargon dropping out of her mouth, which made prospective purchasers dubious about investing money in her?

Perhaps it was her tender years. She had the making, though, of a good worker. She was raw-boned and strong, with muscles which could be trained to a steel-like hardness.

Be that as it may, Mau-Mau will certainly miss her. Here, then, is the answer to her prayer; this her reward for undying confidence in the Almighty: that her child, her last daughter, should be taken away from her in the fading years of her life. Now she will weep truly bitter tears as she sits almost alone under the stars; bitter tears for this baby child who will find a need for Mau-Mau far greater than the mother's need of it.

It is doubtful, however, whether Mau-Mau ever ceased to be philosophical about God's wisdom. "Thy will be done" had been her life's prayer; and this was His will.

§ 2

For Isabella, days at the Nealys' were immediately dismal. One fatal disadvantage was her ignorance of the English language. Fortunately, Mr. Nealy could comprehend something of Isabella's Dutch, but he did not speak a word of the language. Mrs. Nealy, however, neither spoke nor understood Isabella's jargon. To complicate matters, the Nealys had a none-too-friendly hired servant who spoke English, and she, too, had no understanding whatever of the Dutch tongue.

"Go, Bell," Mrs. Nealy would say, "get a frying pan."

The little girl, after trying to guess what her mistress was saying, would scamper off in any direction, and return later, her face querulous and afraid, with a pothook or a plate. If they asked for water, like as not she would bring a dishpan; and a teaspoon was her probable response to a request for a bucket. Her reward in each instance was a beating.

Mrs. Nealy could not under any circumstances bring herself to like Isabella. It may have been the child's unusually masculine appearance, what with her angular bones and her curious low voice. Then there was the language difficulty; and in addition, Isabella held her head a bit too proudly, was very inquisitive and active, seemed always to be peering into something, and already acted with a certain air of independence, as if she imagined that she was destined to be something more than an ordinary slave.

On account of Mrs. Nealy's ill-will, Isabella became the

victim of various hardships. In the winter, her feet were permitted to go uncovered until they were dangerously frozen. Her life was one indignity after another. The worst mishap came one Sunday morning when she received instructions to go to the barn. To her horror, when she arrived there she met her master all ready with a bundle of rods, bound together with cord, to whip her.

There was no delay for the surprised child. First Nealy tied Isabella's hands before her, then he proceeded to the whipping. It is unthinkable that an able-bodied man would unmercifully whip a ten-year-old child for any reason, but whip her Nealy did until deep gashes were cut into her flesh, and the blood streamed from the wounds to the ground below.

All her life Isabella will carry the scars of this beating with her as a remembrance of the occasion. All her life, too, she will carry in her soul a passionate rebelliousness and a yearning to assist any and all people who suffer because Fate has contrived to bring them upon earth under an unlucky star—nurtured in poverty, morally degraded, or cloaked in sable skin.

With what eagerness and anticipation she recalls her mother's admonitions about God! It is at this time that she got into the habit of talking to her Heavenly Being as if He were a person near to her. She asked Him to protect her and to shield her from her persecutors. As conditions got worse she implored Him the more to send information to her whether or not He thought that at a given moment she was doing what accorded with His wishes.

For like most religious folk, she attributed her misfortunes more to her own misdeeds than to the wickedness of her tormentors. Naïvely too, and with that blind insistence of the truly devout, who perceive above every avalanche of disaster a firm haven of security and salvation, Isabella was certain that all her prayers were rewarded fittingly. Had she been badly beaten? That was because she had not known soon enough that a whipping was to come, else by prayer she could have forestalled it. For assuredly, if she but had the time to pray before any calamity, it would never materialize!

Soon enough, however, even she realized that the most effective prayer would be one beseeching complete deliverance from the Nealys with all their horrible English. With the vigor of a robust religious conviction, she set about praying to the Being who comprehended all tongues, imploring Him to send her father to her.

She never doubted that He would hear. Her confidence was rewarded, for lo! one cold winter day, when the snow had fallen, spreading an ermine garment over the wooded hills and in the valleys, a familiar footstep came crunching up the pathway. It was slower and more doddering than formerly, almost groping in its careful, mincing tread, but for Isabella filled with strength and promise. Father!

He probably told her that Mau-Mau had heard her prayers. However, for a long while the two of them talked about everything under the heavens except the thing which was uppermost in Isabella's mind. Such things must not even be whispered too near the presence of one's master, and it was not until father and daughter had walked far down the road to the gate leading out from the Nealy place that Isabella unburdened her heart to Baumfree.

"I'm very anxious about something," she confided to him in the curious Dutch brogue which they were accustomed to employ. "It is terrible here. The Nealys abuse and beat me all the time. If I stay much longer they may really hurt me."

She disclosed to her father's horrified gaze her scars and bruises.

"Can't you help me?" she pleaded. "Maybe you can find

someone who needs a girl. Perhaps he would arrange to buy me."

The distressed father assured her that he would not rest until her prayer was answered. With embittered heart he tore himself away from his bereft child.

Isabella walked back to the house resolved to increase both the tempo and the fervor of her praying.

"Oh, God," she implored the heavens, "help my father to get me a new place, and help him to get me a better place."

Each day she repeated this prayer over and over. And to prove to her Heavenly Father how much more in earnest she was than ever before, she made a daily retreat to the exact spot where her father had shared the common sorrow with her. Then slowly she walked, step after step, in the big shoe tracks which her father had made in the snow after he had taken his departure from her.

Almost any Negro knows what is meant by "Black Dispatch." The idea is a holdover from African days when, by drum wireless, messages were sent from one tribe to another for hundreds of miles. It is a sixth sense. Doubtless Baumfree set the wires hot on his return to the old homestead. The air probably buzzed with the news: "Isabella must be traded. Isabella must be traded."

Not long after, while Isabella was working about the Nealy estate, a man approached and asked her if she would like to go and live with him and his folk. She looked up, with eyes radiant as the sun, into the man's good-tempered, strong, weather-beaten face. She was glad, glad .... more glad by far than surprised. She *knew* that he would come. He was bound to come. This man was the answer to her prayer.

His name was Martin Scriver, and he lived in Kingston, about five miles away from the Nealys. He was a fisherman, but he also was the proprietor of a third-rate tavern and grog shop.

Isabella had no sooner indicated to him that she was willing to accompany him, than he hastened to Nealy and offered him all of one hundred five dollars in cash for her. Nealy probably thought it good riddance, wondering if Scriver realized what he was in for, considering Isabella's Dutch speech and her upstart manners, but he pocketed the money and said little.

Scriver turned homeward, riding horseback. Isabella followed him on foot.

Now life suddenly became a glorious adventure.

Scriver and his family were not worried about differences between slave and master classes. Being in very ordinary circumstances themselves—rollicking seafaring people used to their beer and skittles—their chief interest lay in being simple and honest, well disposed towards all comers, kind to their intimates, and lovers of the out-of-doors.

Like many such folk, they were rough and crude. They had little education, less religion, and no culture. They never made pious utterances, and what they did utter would be as a rule unprintable even in these days of uncensored publication. They let Isabella laugh and sing and dance, and gad about the open creation to her heart's content.

If at times Isabella had appeared brusque or uncouth in the conventional slave atmosphere at John Nealy's, that gentleman and his wife should have come upon her a short while after she had begun to live with these rough folk. Her lithe growing body, inured to life in the open, developed the strength of a green sapling and the hardness of nails, qualities which would remain with her all her long life. Rising early in the morning, running briskly to the wharf where Scriver's fishing boats lay with the night's catch, helping to unload or to row the boats; lugging herbs

and roots for the beers to be sold at the tavern, entering
the fields to hoe the corn, riding horses; again tripping
gaily down to the strand for a gallon of molasses to be
emptied into the liquor, no doubt imbibing some of the
contents at the tavern, Isabella made rapid progress, presumably, in the art of cheery and boisterous living. She
completely forgot her God, learned all manner of perfectly
atrocious habits, including, no doubt, the one of smoking
a pipe, which remained with her for decades—and acquired
in place of her rapidly waning Dutch a brand of English
which for its grammar would have shamed a cockney, and
for its homely vulgarity would have identified her with a
boat's crew.

Now the days were scarcely long enough. One breath
and they had lengthened into weeks; two, and they were
months; in little more than a twinkling, lo! an entire year
and a half had flown. Flown, too, was the demure, sensitive,
and frightened child, who pleaded with God to free her
from her persecutors, then waited, patient and certain, for
the answer to her prayers. Here, instead, was a gawky
creature of about thirteen years, angular of body and strong
as a whiplash, still reminiscent of one in whom is the spark
of regality, black as the night and carefree as the wind.
Undoubtedly she was not pretty, but there was something
about the way she tossed her head, something about the
erect thrust of her body, and something in those wide-open
glances of her eyes and the firm disposition of her lips that
attracted one's attention, and even the admiration of the
senses. You were not likely to give Isabella a glancing look,
then simply pass her by.

John Dumont, a near-by plantation owner, must have
divined something in her to make his heart glad; for he
was not the kind of man to throw away money; yet he
bargained with Scriver for her, and offered—not the one
hundred five dollars which Scriver had paid some months

before—but more than three times that amount—seventy pounds to be exact.

§ 3

The new life began badly.

If it had been left entirely with John Dumont, everything would have been auspicious, notwithstanding the nostalgia which seized upon Isabella after she left Scriver; for Dumont was a kind gentleman, who had been accustomed to slavery and the ways of slaves. True, he was disposed to deal with his human chattel as if they were a superior brand of domestic animal, but it is not over-generous to grant that he was reasonably kind and considerate with them.

Mrs. Dumont, however, was another matter. All her life, up to marriage with Dumont, she had been accustomed to hired servants. She had never lived with slaves, and knew nothing about them. Their idiosyncrasies bothered her. She was annoyed by their indifference to the amenities of life, and by their general casualness about matters which to her were of great moment. It made very little difference to these folk whether they did much work or little. They walked indifferently. They understood indifferently. That these attitudes were frequently feigned in order to escape added arduous duties merely aroused Mrs. Dumont's indignation to white heat.

Isabella, who with her independent manner was quite different from the usual run of slaves, should have become her favorite, as she already was Dumont's, but instead she became her pet anathema. Where Isabella's distinctiveness endeared her to the appreciative Dumont—to Mrs. Dumont, this girl with her airy manners, her confidence and self-assertion was simply a "nigger wench" about to be spoiled by her husband's admiration.

But Isabella was not deterred by Mrs. Dumont's ill will.

She utilized her alert talents to their greatest extent in order to cultivate the stronger friendliness of her master. This infuriated the woman of the house. The more Isabella rose in the favor of John Dumont, the more furiously Mrs. Dumont railed against her. But the master continued to praise her lavishly.

"Why, that girl Isabella," he said, "she can do as much as half a dozen of these others. She is better to me than a man. She will do a large family washing in the night, and be ready in the morning to go into the field and do as much raking and binding as my best hands."

The whole household was aroused by his extravagant praise.

"That's because she is a white folks' nigger!" the other slaves protested under their breath. "She sits up all night working for Marse John; sometimes she just stands up there against the wall and snatches sleep while she's working, and then she starts right out again the next morning working some more. What is to become of all of us if she gets Marse John looking for us to do the same as she?"

Mrs. Dumont was indignant.

"You think she can do an extraordinary amount of work," she remonstrated with her husband, "but that's because you don't look at the kind of work she does. It's never more than half done. You wait and you'll see."

The battle was not long in being decided.

It was Isabella's task to prepare the morning potatoes and place them on the table. Several mornings they had come to the table looking suspiciously dingy.

"Here's a fine specimen of Isabella's work," Mrs. Dumont remarked petulantly. "Just look at these horrible potatoes. This is the way all her work is done."

After a few recurrences, even John Dumont was annoyed. Finally he lost patience.

"Here, Isabella," he said, "you'll have to do better than

this. You're being careless. Take care with these potatoes."

Upon which Kate, the hired servant, hurled a vicious rebuke in Isabella's direction.

Isabella attended to the potatoes as carefully as she knew how. Still they came out of the pan a dingy black instead of the white or brown color she so much desired. Now she was frantic. What trick of fate was this? Had her cunning suddenly left her? And where was God?

The young girl was almost ready to give up when Dumont's daughter Gertrude came to her one evening and secretly consoled her.

"You know, Bell," she said, "I feel awfully sorry for you. I have been watching you trying so hard, and I'm positive those black potatoes are not your fault. I tell you what—tomorrow morning, wake me early. I shall come downstairs, and while you are out milking the cows, I will cook the potatoes. We'll see if they can't be nice and white. I hate to have Poppee and Mommy scolding you all the time."

Early the next morning Isabella came downstairs to put the potatoes in the water to boil. Gertrude, whom she had called, entered the room a little later and sat down in a corner. In a few minutes Isabella left the house in order to milk the cows.

When Kate came into the kitchen she was greatly surprised to see Gertrude.

"Oh," she exclaimed, showing clearly her astonishment, and some perplexity, "don't you want to go outside and do something for me?"

"Not now," the child replied firmly, "I want to sit here awhile."

Nothing to do but to go on with the work, thought Kate. She piddled around for a few moments, then took a broom and swept about the fire. Suddenly, under cover as she thought, she caught up a chip, lifted some ashes with it, and dashed these into the pot which contained the potatoes. Gertrude had seen enough.

She rushed out of the kitchen, screaming at the top of her voice, "Oh Poppee, oh Poppee, it's Kate. She has been putting ashes in among the potatoes. I just saw her do it."

Her father rushed into the kitchen.

"See all those ashes that fell on the outside of the kettle," said Gertrude. "No wonder the potatoes look dirty every morning, even though Bell washes them clean."

At first Kate had tried to prevent the child's outcries, but Gertrude simply shouted louder to everyone within earshot. When Mr. and Mrs. Dumont arrived, the servant stood about guiltily, with her head hanging in shame. Mrs. Dumont, who would have given anything to quiet her daughter, looked on blankly. Dumont uttered an oath, and pretended that he was very angry. Actually he was tremendously happy. He always did believe in that doughty Isabella!

§ 4

Trouble and sorrow.

Mau-Mau-Bett never entirely recovered from the loss of her two youngest children. For a while she labored patiently by the side of her husband, eking out a bare subsistence. The nights around the fire were dreadfully lonely; she could hardly bear to look up at the stars.

"Oh Lord, how long, how long!"

Too long had she dwelt in the damp cellar. Fever sores began to develop in one of her limbs. Palsy shook her whole body. Gradually her health declined.

What poor creatures you were, Mau-Mau and Baumfree (she called him James), doddering along, picking up a crumb of food here, a stick of wood there, and adding these to the mites which other old slaves nearly as stricken as you contributed in order to keep the wolf from your door!

One morning early in the fall, Baumfree started out to do a few chores for some of the neighbors. Mau-Mau called out to him.

"I'm going to make a loaf of rye bread for you," she said, "and then get Mrs. Simmons to bake it for us. She is baking this afternoon."

"Good!" James answered her. "Before I commence raking the ground, I will knock down some of the apples on that tree yonder, and if you can get some of them baked with the bread it will make a nice relish for our dinner."

After he had beaten down the apples, Mau-Mau came along from out of the cellar and gathered them up. Then Baumfree went on to his other chores.

When he heard the horn announcing that dinner time had arrived, he turned his slow steps homeward, then groped his way into the dark cellar, joyfully anticipating the delicious dish which he had helped to prepare. However, he seemed to observe that the odor of freshly baked bread was absent; and he could not find a trace of the baked apples. What was wrong? Something seemed very strange and cheerless in that cellar. It was peculiarly silent.

He felt his way, with his staff before him, into the room. Suddenly he stumbled over something. He heard an ominous gurgling sound; then something very low and choking. He leaped over the obstacle.

"Lord," he gasped, as he made out the prostrate form of Mau-Mau-Bett.

She had fallen in a fit of palsy, and lay helpless and senseless on the damp floor.

Frantically the nearly helpless old man did everything he could for her, but of what use? Mau-Mau was worn out; worn out with toil; worn out with grief; tired.

She never came to. In a few hours she had died.

See Baumfree on his knees, nearly prostrate with grief

before the corpse of his wife—penniless, lame, feeble, quite blind . . . . and all alone.

Oh, yes, he had his two children. They were some distance away, but not so far that they could not come to the funeral. But after that, what?

They came. Miserable ceremony that it was, Isabella and Peter arrived to perform their last obligation to their beloved Mau-Mau. They were even permitted to stay a few days with their father, now nearly crazy with grief and terror.

"Why, why did not God take me first?" the poor man moans. "Mau-Mau was so much smarter than I. She could get about and take care of herself, but I am so old and helpless. What is to become of me, Isabella? I cannot do anything any longer. All of you children are gone from me. Here I am left helpless and alone."

The broken wreck of a man wept as if his heart were pouring out.

"You will get permission to come and see me sometime, Isabella," he pleaded, "won't you?"

"Of course," his distracted daughter promised him.

The old man continued to weep. He never ceased weeping. The slave daughter had to leave him all alone, just so.

Though she lived only a few miles away from the old Hardenbergh estate, Isabella saw her father only a few times more. It would have been different, no doubt, if trams or trains had been running in her day. But for one who gets about by walking, and only occasionally on horseback, a few miles is almost an entire continent.

The last time Isabella and Baumfree saw each other, she found him seated all alone on a rock by the side of a road, far away from any house. He was making his slow way from the home of one Hardenbergh family to another.

His hair was white like wool. He was almost completely blind, and his creeping gait was like that of an old dray

horse kept on the road long after it should have been re-
tired to clover. However, since the weather was warm
and pleasant, he was enjoying his trip despite his infirmities.

Isabella called out to him, and instantly he recognized
her voice. Naturally he was overjoyed.

She assisted him to the wagon which had carried her
to him, and together they returned for the last time to the
old cellar which used to be home for the entire family.

All along the way the old man never ceased sorrowing.

"All of you have been taken away from me," he whined.
"Now I don't have anyone even to give me so much as a
cup of cold water. Why should I live? Why should I not
die?"

"But," Isabella reminded him gently, addressing him in
the old Dutch of her early childhood, "even if I cannot be
with you, I do love you. Continue to live until better times
come. The white folk say that the state is going to free all
the slaves in another ten years. Only ten years, father,"
she added with the easiest sense of conviction, "and then
I can come and care for you. I will take care of you just
like Mau-Mau-Bett did."

"But my child," her less sanguine father protested, "I
cannot live that long."

But what is the passage of years to a child of fifteen who,
despite whippings, grueling labor, and inconceivable
physical and mental torture, imagines that life is eternal
and old age a myth?

"Oh, do, daddy, do live!" the exuberant young thing
cried, like the members of those modern cults who believe
that if only you will affirm, you can attain any desired
end, "and I will take such good care of you."

However, the disillusioned old man merely shook his
head vacantly.

Meanwhile Dumont became Isabella's idol. He was, in
fact, God.

She imagined that Dumont could see her at all times, and that there was not anything she did or thought which he did not know about in advance. On this account she would go to him, making voluntary confession of her misdemeanors, lest he swoop down upon her on his own account and punish her. How severely he could punish when he wanted to, she had discovered one day when he whipped her for tormenting a household cat.

Her mother had taught her well, religiously. Like that now deceased woman, Isabella readily accepted the relative positions of master and slave without trying to perceive any injustice in that relationship. With all her intelligence and independence, she nevertheless continued to believe that slavery was right and honorable.

There is nothing really astonishing about this. Everyone knows many persons to-day who persist in the belief that industrial serfdom of a kind is God-ordained. Isabella looked down contemptuously upon anyone who decried the injustice of slavery in precisely the way in which these persons scorn individuals who are accused of Communist leanings. It is risky to one's job to be heard or seen sympathizing with Communism. It was risky to speak against slavery in front of Isabella. She was apt to think that it was her God-given duty to report the matter to the proper authorities.

Also, like conventional believers in all ages, Isabella made little or no distinction between preachment by the master to the slave, and inconsistent practice by the master of the things he insisted that the slaves should scrupulously observe. For, in her mind, God and the institutions of this world were so interrelated as to be practically synonymous. Had not her mother taught her so?

But her God was no *spirit*, strange and intangible. He was a man, not a great deal different from Dumont; in fact, Dumont was strangely like God. Did he not jot down in a great book every action of his slaves, to keep as a record? Did he not order one about, and reward when one was good, or punish when evil arose? Yes, Dumont was like God. Only God was a still bigger person, like Napoleon or Lafayette .... and he did live way up there in the sky!

When she had been with Mau-Mau-Bett she had learned a story about a soldier who, after being wounded in battle, was left behind, helpless and starving, by his fleeing comrades. There was nothing left for him to do but pray, and he did this so long that the ground on which he knelt became hard. After that, succor arrived. Isabella imagined that if she would find some place out in the open under the sky where she could speak in loud tones to this Being up in the heavens, she, too, could be heard. Wasn't this the way to combat Mrs. Dumont's evil designs?

She must have a sanctuary.

Near the Dumont house there was a small stream in which an islet covered with much willow shrubbery would provide just such a place. The grazing sheep had made gentle winding paths there, and near by tiny falls of silver water tinkled beneath the huge willow branches which protected everything on the isle from the sun. It was a lonely spot and a lovely one, an ideal place for retirement and peace. And the noisy waterfalls encouraged loud speaking to one's God.

To this place daily, then, and sometimes more frequently, Isabella resorted, alone. In order to assure seclusion for herself, she pulled away branches of the shrubbery from the center and wove them together to form a wall on the outside, thus constructing a circular arched alcove entirely of graceful willows. Here she communed with God as if she were talking to her father. Here she prayed.

She would begin with the Lord's Prayer, still chanted in the Dutch patois which her mother had taught her; and

then to God she would relate all her troubles and suffer-
ings in the most personal manner and in minute detail.

She spared neither herself nor the Almighty. In one
moment she was begging forgiveness for some piece of
wrongdoing; in the next she commanded God as if he
were her father or brother. For, as a matter of fact, she
assumed that God was more greatly indebted to her than
she to him.

She cultivated, also, the habit of exchanging promises
with God.

"You help me out of this piece of trouble, God," she
would say, "and I will pay you back by being a good girl."

And like all free and easy promisers, she discovered that
it was far more simple to make a promise than to fulfill one.

An easy way out of that!

"Of course, God," she would cajole Him, "you realize
that much as I would like to keep my part of the bargain,
this is impossible under the circumstances; but if you will
remedy this present difficulty, you will see whether I won't
do all that I have promised. And just to show you I mean
what I say, I shall be good all day tomorrow. . . . But you
must be sure to help me!"

Whereupon she again promptly forgot all about her
promise.

Her actions and mannerisms were those of a child; but
her inclination towards the mystical and religious was a
direct heritage from the days when she lived with her
mother. It is a question whether she ever would have
been led into the paths leading up to the important activities of her later life if she had not received these impulses
so forcefully in her most impressionable years.

It was these influences which made it easy for her, despite her naturally commanding manner, to accept the one-
sided morality of the master class, and not to resent it
except in the case of persons who themselves were beyond
the pale—such as Mrs. Dumont.

But she did not possess that imperious disposition of hers, nor her great love of free activity and desire to be well up in God's councils, merely to accept forever without question all of life's rebuffs. Some of these debatable issues were bound to cut under and into the sheath of her soul; she would not and could not forever accept them so readily. Indeed, she *will* question, she *will* assert a difference of opinion; and finally she will break out in open rebellion.

Her eyes began to be stripped of a certain blind acquiescence by one of the early tragedies of her young life.

Not far away from the Dumont household an Englishman by the name of Catlin had an estate. On this place was a slave called Robert, who became acquainted with Isabella and grew to love her. Isabella, too, fell in love with him.

Catlin, however, had other ideas. Should Robert marry Isabella, their children would be added to the human chattel on Dumont's estate rather than on his own. This was a palpable waste of human seed!

"You are not ever to go over to Dumont's in order to visit that girl," Catlin commanded Robert. "If you want a wife, then take one of the women on this plantation."

In love matters, Robert was no different from Romeos the world over. All the protestations of the master class to the contrary notwithstanding, he was not impressed. If he could not visit his Juliet with his master's permission, then he must visit her clandestinely. God willing, he intended to make this woman his bride.

For a while he managed affairs very successfully. Then one Saturday afternoon, having heard that Isabella was ill, he decided to pay her a broad daylight visit. Isabella was unaware of his intentions.

That afternoon John Dumont took the trouble to come to her sick room and ask her if she had seen anything of Robert.

"No, I have not," she replied.

"Well, if you do see him," Dumont cautioned her, "tell him to take care of himself, for the Catlins are after him."

Robert made his appearance in the distance almost the instant Dumont uttered this admonition. Isabella could discern him through the window of her sick room but, before he could reach her and be warned, Catlin and his son also had appeared. She saw with horror that they had overtaken him.

The slave's masters were filled with the infinite rage of persons bent upon discovering the condition they protest against. The elder Catlin hurled a vehement oath at Robert, then turned to his son and called out, "Knock down the black rascal."

Both of them fell on the slave with their canes and attacked him as if he had been a marauding wolf. With the heavy ends of their sticks they beat him until his face and head were almost pulpy. The blood streamed down from him as if he were a beast being slaughtered.

Dumont, who had rushed from Isabella's room, called out to them, "Get away from here. You can't spill human blood on my premises any longer. I'll have no niggers killed here."

The Catlins, now that they were frustrated in their original intention, drew out a rope and tied the hands of the helpless victim so tightly that Dumont had to interfere again.

"Loosen them," he insisted. "I would not permit even a brute to be tied in this manner."

With his hands tied behind him, the helpless slave was driven home. Dumont followed behind, doubtless for Isabella's sake, in order that no further harm might befall her lover.

Robert, however, was completely subdued. He never visited Isabella again. Soon after the horrible affair, he did as he had been commanded, and married a woman on his own estate.

The shock of this experience, together with the sense of her impotence in a situation which so vitally involved her, began at last to shake the foundation of Isabella's lone faith—a faith that had been imbibed from her mother, to color her life completely, up through the period of her idolatry of Dumont.

Isabella married also.

The "preacher" performed the usual slave ceremony for her and a slave called Thomas, and thus they became man and wife.

Thomas had been married two times previously, but what had happened to his former wives we are unable to say. It is possible that they had died. The more probable fact is that they had been separated and sold apart from their husband. Apparently he was considerably older than Isabella, for a few years later we discover him, a lonely old freedman, so decrepit and poor that about the year 1830 he is forced to enter an almshouse, where a short time later he passes away.

Whether Isabella and her husband separated for other reasons than the vicissitudes of slavery, and whether or not Isabella could have saved him from such a dismal end, we have no sure way of knowing. Isabella's husband is one of the forgotten men. He was the father of five children but, considering Isabella's attitude towards Dumont, it seems likely that they were less the children of Thomas than of Dumont. With what obvious delight Isabella displays these new tokens of wealth in the estate of her master!

Dumont, it must be admitted, transferred his admiration for Isabella to her children. If he entered his home and found one of the little ones crying—especially if Isabella was too busy attending to the needs of Mrs. Dumont to pay any heed to her own—he would indignantly reprove his wife.

"Why don't you see to it that the child is taken care of?" he would shout at her. "I will not have this crying. I cannot bear it. I will not hear any child cry so."

Then turning to Isabella he would say, "Here, Bell, take care of this child even if you don't do any more work for a week."

And he would remain in the room to see to it that Mrs. Dumont did not attempt to countermand his instructions.

It was some time after one of her children was born that Isabella walked twelve miles, with the infant in her arms, in order to pay her father another visit. His failing eyesight probably would prevent him from seeing the little one, but what grandparent would not be happy to take in his arms the child of his child?

However, when Isabella had arrived at the place where she thought she would find him, she learned that he had just departed for a place which was another twenty miles distant. That was too much for the already weary mother and child. Isabella had to turn back.

She never saw her father again.

That man had clung too long to life. Even the Hardenberghs grew tired of him. They began to scheme to get rid of him.

When Mau-Mau-Bett died, she left a brother named Caesar, whose wife was called Betsey. They were useless old slaves by this time, who like Baumfree would be less expense if they were granted their freedom. Caesar was racked with fever sores; Betsey was seared with jaundice. Death probably would have been the most welcome thing in the world to them—except freedom.

One day some of the Hardenberghs called to them and

asked, "What would you say about having your freedom, provided you took care of Baumfree?"

Helpless as they were, the magic word "freedom" still charmed the pitiable old creatures. Oblivious of the destitution to which they were assigning themselves, they eagerly agreed to the bargain.

The Hardenberghs had a rude cabin far off from any neighboring place. Here they set down the three miserable old people. Their destitution was pathetic. Baumfree had thought himself badly off before, but now he would fare far worse; for these decrepit shadows whom the Hardenberghs had provided to be his guardians could not keep the wolf away from their own door, much less take care of a third person. That was not the worst, however. Betsey died soon after she was freed, only to be followed by Caesar a short while later. Here now was Baumfree, absolutely alone. For him the mills of the gods were grinding exceeding fine.

His body was crusted with dirt. Vermin infested his ragged clothing. He was too feeble to provide for himself, or to take care of his bodily needs. No one would help him; no one could help him.

An aged Negro woman, formerly a slave named Soan, came over to visit him one day. He petitioned her to assist him.

"Soan, Soan," he cried out to her, his grief making it difficult for him to speak, "do stay awhile. Stay awhile, Soan, and please wash me and mend these tatters."

The sympathizing old woman looked over at him, considering long and deeply whether she should accede to his entreaty. She was so old and feeble that it would not take much to send her to her grave.

She groaned.

"I dare not," she replied. "I would surely get sick. . . . I cannot."

She tarried awhile, comforting him as well as a feeble old person could. Then she left him.

Fortunately for Baumfree, he did not live long after this experience. One chilly morning some passer-by stumbling into his miserable shack found him on his straw pallet, frozen stiff. The blasts of winter had touched him, at last, with the sceptre of freedom.

Now that the faithful servant was dead, John Hardenbergh, who had tired of caring for him in life, could not find encomium extravagant enough for him.

"An ever kind and faithful slave he was," he said mournfully.

Turning to the prostrate form, he addressed the corpse.

"Baumfree," he said, "now you shall have a good funeral."

The negligent master signified by these remarks that Baumfree should have a coffin made entirely of pine wood covered with black paint, instead of the usual one of plain rough boards.

The mourners also should receive special consideration. They might drown their sorrows in the whiskey contained in a big jug which he presented to them as a special token to the memory of a faithful servant.

§ 5

Years have passed.

Isabella is a woman in her late twenties. For her too, now, time is weighing heavily. Nearly ten years she has been waiting for July 4, 1827, when, according to a law passed in 1817, she would be made a free woman. Dumont has promised to grant her an extra year of freedom if she serves him faithfully, but the promised day of freedom is all too slow in arriving.

Then just a year or so before the time agreed upon for

her release, Isabella contracted a disease in her hand which hampered her in her work. She toiled as well as she could under the handicap but Dumont, who was loath to part with such a good servant, seized upon her disability as a pretext for retaining her the extra year.

The more Isabella pleaded for her freedom, the more inflexible Dumont became in his determination to hold her up to the last minute provided by the law. Never had he realized so deeply how valuable a servant he was letting go from him. On the market she would bring a fancy price; it was ridiculous to relinquish her for absolutely nothing. What if there had been a promise? Was there such a thing as a valid promise where a slave was involved?

Isabella tried to think through her predicament. Dumont's resort to subterfuge was to be expected from a slaveowner. These masters who trained their slaves to idolize them and their principles were just like that. If you will do thus and so, they say, we promise to give you this and that; but when the time comes for fulfilling the contract, they recollect nothing. Will you force them? At your peril. Perhaps you will be told that you failed to perform your part; or in the case of more brutal masters, you are just a plain liar.

Or even worse.

There was Master Charles Brodhead. He had promised his slave Ned that when harvesting was over he might go to see his wife who lived on another estate more than twenty miles away. Ned, taking his master at his word, worked early and late until the harvest was cleared. Then he claimed as his part of the contract arrangement the privilege of visiting his wife.

"You misunderstood," said Charles Brodhead, archly. "I merely claimed that I would *see* if you could go to your wife after the harvest was over. But now I see that I cannot let you go."

Ned was determined to force the promise. There was

nothing criminal about going to see one's wife, and what could be more natural or desirable? The slave proceeded to clean his shoes as if preparing to go somewhere.

His master, curious about this behaviour, asked him, "You do not intend to go without my permission, do you?"

"Yes," Ned replied very quietly. "You made me your promise, and now you can keep that promise."

"Very well," answered the master; but thereupon he took up a stick that lay near him and struck Ned such a terrific blow on the head that he broke his skull, killing him instantly.

Isabella reflected well and long over the possibility of some similar eventuality to her desire to procure her freedom. Her mind inclined her to play along safely with her master, especially since the state would grant her freedom in just a year more. But her increasing will urged her to be her own mistress in the matter. The battle raged awhile; then she made her decision.

"I shall pin about one hundred pounds more of wool for Master John," she thought to herself, "then I shall take my leave."

The queen would act upon her prerogatives even if it were best to take a circuitous route. Later she will be more direct.

She had no fear of suffering Ned's fate, for in her mind it was clear that God intended no such end for her. Who could be afraid of Dumont who was not afraid of God? For this proud woman, not satisfied merely with demanding her part of the bargain with Dumont, proceeded to the highest tribunal and laid down the law.

"Oh, God," she broke forth in a recently acquired, quaint English which from now on will never forsake her, "I been a-askin' you, an' askin' you, an' askin' you, for all this long time to make my massa an' missis better, an' you don't do it; an' what *can* be the reason? .... Why—maybe you *can't!* Well, I shouldn't wonder if you couldn't. Well, now, I tell you, I'll make a bargain with you. Ef you'll help me to git away from my massa an' missis, I'll agree to be good; but ef you don't help me, I really don't think I can be."

She is putting her religion to the pragmatic test. No more blind faith!

"Now," she continued, "I want to git away; but the trouble's jest been, ef I try to git away in the night, I can't see; an' ef I try to git away in the daytime, they'll see me an' be after me."

She waited for an answer to her prayer. Probably she was just as confident that the response would come as she had been when she begged to be freed from John Nealy; but certainly she was in no mood to have her wishes crossed or denied. She lifted her thoughts heavenward, transferring herself in her imagination within earshot of the Almighty.

A short while afterwards she thought she actually heard the Lord suggesting to her, "Get up two or three hours before daylight, and start off."

She was entirely prepared for the response to her appeal. "Thank you, Lord," she replied, "that's a good idea."

She did not hesitate. One fine fall morning, about three o'clock, she arose and prepared to leave. In a big cotton handkerchief she put together some articles of clothing and food; then with this in one hand and an infant on her arm she stepped stealthily, in all likelihood barefooted, from the rear of Dumont's home. Away she rushed until, by the time a brilliant autumn sun cast its splendor all about, she had gained the summit of a hill a considerable distance from the Dumont home.

The gleaming rays spread all about her, scattering golden hues on the leaves and in the valley down below. Never before had she felt the sun so bright. A mixed feeling of

joy and alarm came over her. How good to be free....
free!

But suppose they pursued her! She looked cautiously
about her. No one was in sight. She sat down for a few
moments to feed her infant. Then she kneeled down on
the ground and prayed once more to God.

"Well, Lord," she called out, with that unaffected intimacy which was always her manner, "you started me out;
now please show me where to go."

This bold woman, guilty of the most serious crime in
the calendar of slave offenses, had never once considered
where she would seek refuge!

She did know a friendly person near by whose name
was Levi Rowe. To his home she repaired, and there she
asked him to help her out of her difficulty. Rowe urged
her to proceed to the home of a certain Van Wagener
some miles away, where he was sure she would receive a
hospitable greeting.

Traveling on foot, and laden with the child as she was,
it took her from early morning until far into the night
to reach her destination. She had no exact acquaintance
with the Van Wagener home, but, imaginative as always,
she was confident she would recognize the house from a
dream she had had recently.

"That's the place for me," she said to herself when she
had come up to a house which fitted her impression of the
one she had dreamed about. "I'll stop here."

Mr. and Mrs. Isaac Van Wagener were not at home, but
an elderly mother received her very kindly, and permitted
her to await their arrival. When they had returned,
she related to them the story of Isabella, to which
they listened very sympathetically. Immediately they offered employment to Isabella in their own home, and, as if
this were not sufficient evidence of their generous hearts,
they set about right away to make her a member of the

household. They set her down at the table to supper; then, that meal finished, they led her to a room which contained a tall white bed. This they told her was to be her room.

Incredible as it seems, Isabella had never slept in a bed before. Therefore, this unexpected turn of events in the Van Wagener household frightened her more, probably, than her precipitate flight from her former master. Was there not some mistake? She had appealed to her God for freedom, but she had not intended these trimmings! Certainly the Van Wageners could not mean that she should sleep in this bed! If they did—well, she could not bring herself to it. Instead, observing the habits which had been cultivated through years of slavery, she crept underneath the bed, and there on the floor fell fast asleep.

It is easy to imagine Mrs. Van Wagener's surprise when the next morning she entered Isabella's room to inquire of her health, and discovered the bed untouched.

"Why, Isabella," the astonished woman gasped, "didn't you sleep last night?"

"Yes," Isabella replied, with the air of a little girl who, on her first excursion away from home, wonders why a particular practice which has become second nature with her should cause consternation, "I never slept better."

"Well," Mrs. Van Wagener admonished her, "you haven't been in the bed!"

So they did mean that bed for her!

"Lord, ma'am," Isabella fairly shrieked, "you didn't think of such a thing as me sleeping on that there bed, did you? I never heard of such a thing in my life!"

She had purposely placed only a few miles' distance between herself and Dumont. The old line of duty which her mother had drilled into her still influenced all her actions. God would not be pleased if she made a lot of trouble for Dumont, who was sure to search for her.

It was one thing to seize one's liberty, especially when that had been promised. It was quite a different thing to create unnecessary vexation for one's former master. In matters like this one, one must play fair. She actually awaited Dumont's coming!

Nor had she long to wait. He came for her just as she knew he would, hoping if not expecting to take her back.

Undoubtedly the formalities were very brief. Isabella and Dumont knew each other too well to engage in rigmarole.

"Well, Bell," Dumont began, "so you've run away from me."

"No," the former slave calmly replied, "I did *not* run away. I walked away by daylight, and all because you promised me a year of my time."

He wasted no words refuting her unwelcome logic.

"You must go back with me," he said, laconically.

But Isabella informed him in no mistaken tones, "No, I won't go back with you."

"Well, then," Dumont continued, evidently prepared for this eventuality, "I shall take the child. It belongs to me."

"Indeed, you shall not," Isabella cried out with emphasis.

At this moment, Isaac Van Wagener, who had overheard some of the conversation, appeared.

"Mr. Dumont," he interrupted, "I do not believe in slavery. I never buy or sell human beings. This time, however, rather than have Isabella taken away by force, suppose I buy her services for the balance of the year? I will give you twenty dollars for her services, and five dollars additional for the infant's services."

Dumont must have thought this a queer kind of bargain; but then Isabella was a queer kind of person. It did not take him long to accept Van Wagener's proposal.

"Master!" Isabella cried out to her benefactor.

"No, no, not that," Van Wagener exclaimed. "Do not

call me or anyone 'master.' There is but one master; and He who is your master is my master. Call me Isaac Van Wagener, and my wife Maria Van Wagener."

Dumont probably imagined that he was in the house of a mad man. Even Isabella, accustomed by this time to the unconventionality of the Van Wagener household, could not quite understand this departure from custom. But we may be very certain that this principle which Van Wagener had laid down as the rule of his house did not dampen her belief that the Master who was both Van Wagener's master and her own was a mighty being with an endless treasure of gifts which she could turn to account.

§ 6

The assured freedom, however, did not satisfy her.

Before many months, she was so much the victim of nostalgia—for Dumont had been a prince of masters as masters went—that her will engaged in a struggle to return to Dumont which was as intense as her previous struggle had been to obtain freedom. Life now was too certain, too placid, and she longed for some of the exciting adventures which on the Dumont plantation she had imagined were making her life miserable. She was in conflict with her own nature.

From her parents Isabella had inherited a robust constitution, an inquisitive mind, and a roving spirit. Her mother had inculcated a devotion to duty and a loyalty to convention, on the one hand, and a belief in the infinite power of God on the other. Living with the Scrivers, she had cultivated her body; her mind and will developed in an atmosphere of extraordinary freedom; and she learned what it is to take delight in the world of things. At the Dumonts' there was much less freedom, but such deprivations as she endured served to accentuate the utility of a certain mystical element in her nature, which Mau-

Mau-Bett had spared no pains to emphasize. Thus her strong body became lost, temporarily, underneath a thick coating of mysticism.

If life became hard at the Dumonts', or mystifying, or even impossible, she always had her woodland retreat where in her imagination she could soar at will to the outer heavens of hope and desire. When, on the other hand, contact with the spiritual forces palled, there were the holidays, especially Christmas, Easter, and Independence Day, when she and the other slaves might let their senses have free rein in a round of pleasure and conviviality.

But here at the Van Wageners' all was peace and quiet. These staid folk took their Bible literally, and if they did not believe in persecuting black folk, neither did they have any use for excesses of any kind, whether they were of a pleasurable or painful variety.

We can be sure that Isabella, now a woman of nearly thirty years, who had emerged first from the mystified child of ten years into the crude, robust, swearing, swashbuckling lass of thirteen, later to become the favorite maid-servant of John Dumont, was no Puritan. Else, how could she have separated from her husband, even if, as we believe, he dissented from her idea of running away from her master? And if this does not seem to prove anything, then account for the fact that she left all but one of her children on the estate from which she fled. Before many moons she will pay dearly for having put personal preference ahead of family responsibilities; and none more than she, probably, will ascribe part of the troubles arising out of her flight to an innate paganism which up to now might flare up at any time.

In Isabella we see well demonstrated the psychological complexity of the American-Negro mind which frequently makes it difficult for the Anglo-Saxon to arrive at a fair sense of understanding or appreciation. Religion would seem to be an absolutely essential phase of the Negro's constitution; but it is only a phase, or rather it is one aspect of his essentially expressive personality. Another aspect is joy, or perhaps the French have expressed it better—*joie de vivre*. Where the Anglo-Saxon Puritan, on the one hand, loses all sense of proportion between moral demands and the right of man to enjoy life, and on the other hand libertines go quite to the other extreme and lose all moral restraint, the Negro in nine cases out of ten takes his religion quite as seriously as the Anglo-Saxon Puritan, but substitutes exuberance and joy for asceticism. The result is that while the Puritan is in danger of an overdose of morbidity and neurosis, the Negro is more apt to develop a quite healthy paganism. Thus the Negro's religion may be an outlet for his emotion, but it is never a stop-gap, as is so frequently the case with the Anglo-Saxon. It fits in with his mercurial temperament, which demands a reasonable balance in the observance of Nature's (that is, "God's") laws, with elbowroom to enjoy an untrammelled moment of sheer ecstasy.

It was this balance which Isabella felt she was missing in the home of the Van Wageners. We say "felt" in order to suggest merely a mild sense of awareness on her part, for Isabella both by endowment and precept was even more disposed towards the mystical than is the average Negro. Temperamentally she might have been a good-natured Cotton Mather. Later in life she will want to save the world from moral damnation; she will preach fire and brimstone, and warn men of the perils of wickedness. Her particular wrath will be poured down upon the slave-owning class. She will mean serious business; but always a superabundance of humor, a rich emotional surplusage, will steer her clear of the Puritan's error, namely, to convert the heathen to a belief in Christianity, come what may to love and all of the amenities of life; and instead she will utilize love to smooth away sin and inhumanity.

For the present, however, the seeming contradiction of

her spiritual aspiration and pagan sensitiveness will delay in her a clear understanding of the relation between her true self and her mission in life; but the early training under her mother is sure to keep her pagan-drawn star from flying out of its moral orbit.

Now she imagines that anything is preferable to the drab and uninteresting life of the cultured home of the Van Wageners. Day by day she strains at the leash—not outwardly, so that the Van Wageners might be aware or annoyed, but, what is worse for a person of her ir-repressible temperament, inwardly.

As one of the festival days approached, her body burned to be back with her Negro friends, mixing in their frivolous fun, joining in their hilarity and their open licentiousness. Hourly she pined for just another taste of "fun," full-grown woman though she was—yea, wife, and mother of five children—in spite of everything that her experience, unusual even for a slave, had contributed to a sobering philosophical attitude.

At last she could contain herself no longer. She would explode if she did not express the truth which was con-suming her. One morning she presents herself to Mrs. Van Wagener, and prepares the way for a hasty departure. Note, however, that alloyed with her earthly passion to return to the flesh-pots of Egypt is an intuitive, meta-physical, or shall we say mystical element in her temper-ament, which leads her to announce to Mrs. Van Wagener not, "I am going to leave you and go back to Mr. Dumont," but instead, "My master, Dumont, is coming today for me, and I shall return with him."

Observe also how in her fall from the higher grace she has reverted to the deferential attitude, "master."

Of course, the Van Wageners are surprised, and they wonder whether they are harboring a partly insane person or merely a trickster.

"And how did you come by such information?" they ask.

Isabella answers them in a fashion absolutely typical of the woman throughout her life.

"No one told me," she says quietly. "I just feel that he will come."

Now the strange thing about all this (though Africans accustomed to Black Magic might not consider it strange) is that Dumont did come to the house that very day. For what reason we do not know; certainly not to fetch Isabella. Evidently he had had enough of this strange creature by this time for, when she informed him that she would accompany him on his return home, he replied in words to this effect, "Not on your life. I shall not take you back again. You ran away from me."

But Isabella was not deterred by his words. She knew the man too well to be affected by anything he might say; and besides, she did not believe that he meant one word of what he had said. She therefore proceeded to make herself ready, took her child in her arms and, as soon as she saw her former master seat himself in his carriage, she advanced towards him with the intention of seating herself in the rear of the vehicle, and going back with him.

Then a strange thing happened. With all the suddenness of a flash of lightning, God revealed Himself to her. (Could she recently have been impressed with the story of Saul of Tarsus?) In an instant God was over everything.... there was no place where God was not.... she had been a great sinner to forget her almighty Friend who had been ever ready to help her in trouble.

Now she wanted to escape from that sea of unfulfilled promises which she had poured out to Him, memories of which surged through her mind like restless billows. Her soul appeared just a tissue of lies, and she shrank in terror from the gaze of the Being whom all her life she had been addressing with such easy familiarity. She wished to hide herself where she could not be seen or found, but she realized now that there was no place, not even Hell, where He was not.

Her frightened mind conjures up the most cruel punishments for herself, and she stands at attention for just one more look of His to extinguish her life much as one snuffs out a candle. She feels empty and panicky; she grovels like a person who knows he is about to be suffocated; a minute more and her flame will be extinguished.

But she was not snuffed out.

Greatly to her relief, when she had returned to a more normal emotional state, she awakened to find herself still alive. Dumont, however, had gone, actually and symbolically.

She would never have need again for holidays and worldly pleasures. Henceforth and forever more she would give everything to God and everything for God. She would laugh? Of course. Sing? Most certainly. Dance? Perhaps. But all for God; all in the name of God. We shall see her soon, enmeshed in one of the most curious God-dedicated affairs ever to be recorded in the annals of American religious experience. Everything in the category of worship and crime will be involved: mock piety, theft, love, frivolity, carnality—even murder, perhaps; but as far as Isabella is concerned it will all have been for God.

Her expression as she left the spot where Dumont had been sitting and rushed into the home of the Van Wageners, exclaiming, "Oh, God, I did not know you were so big!" is symbolic of the restlessness which her soul from now on will experience wherever it resides, whatever it is occupied about. As a rule, the activity in which she is engaged will appear in itself insignificant; the cause which engrosses her mind at a given moment will prove too single; her limbs, restless like those of a race horse, will whisk her about here, there, everywhere. That mind of hers will be busy with thoughts and plans on a dozen different matters at once; she will reach down into the gutters where besotted drunkards wallow in crime, or recently freed black men flounder about in ignorance, on up to the hallowed room where one of the greatest presidents of a great republic teeters on the edge of a spiritual abyss, and carves out for himself a name in eternity.

A decided change came over Isabella. The chances are that had she reached this point in her spiritual development a year sooner, she would have remained, at any cost, with her husband and children, no matter how impatient she was to leave the Dumont estate. Now she is obsessed with an almost paralyzing anxiety to find out all about Jehovah. In her conscience-stricken shame, however, she hesitates even to pray to Him.

"What!" she cries out in her anguish, "shall I lie again to God? I have told Him nothing but lies; and shall I speak again, and tell another lie to God?"

It may have been at this time that she attended one of the first religious meetings of her life; for, unusual as it may seem, she herself is authority for the statement that she did not attend a church meeting until after her emancipation. This meeting, chiefly of white persons, was held in a private house, and Isabella, unaccustomed to such places, was so fearful about entering that she stood outside, peering in at the open window.

The minister took as his text, "Behold I come quickly, and my reward is with me to give to every man according as his work shall be." It was the first time Isabella had heard a text from Scripture quoted in this way, and the words and the sermon made a profound impression on her. It was the first time, too, that she heard the words of a hymn called "The Holy City," and as she listened by the window to the preacher reading the hymn and lining it for his congregation, she found herself engraving the words on her mind and its sentiments in her heart.

Out of her awareness of great spiritual need comes, in its own peculiar way, the significant realization of an intercessor who can plead her case with God. She must have heard something about Jesus before this time, but presumably her mind had been too much engrossed with purely personal and material matters for her to comprehend the spiritual significance of this cornerstone of Christian belief. Now when she understood her profound need of someone worthy enough to intercede for her before the Almighty, someone who would plead for her out of the purity of his own life, and who would apprise her God of her own sense of unworthiness and her equally great desire to repent of former misdeeds, it recurred to her mind that Christians did have just such a one who represented them before the bar of heaven.

She racks her soul for the answer to her great problem. Who might this intercessor be? A girl friend? Mr. or Mrs. Van Wagener? Levi Rowe? Nonsense. These were all too much in her own predicament. No more hero worship such as she had known in the Dumont era. No, this was some completely different being.

As with many individuals who are experiencing an emotional crisis of this kind, she soars far above mere earthly routine, and peers into the heavens for visions of the new creation.

"Who are you?" she exclaims, as she perceives the vision brightening and forming itself distinctly before her gaze.

She seems to be dwelling in an entirely foreign world. All about her is an atmosphere of holiness, of love, and of purity. A quiet ecstatic sensation closes in about her. Her heart seems singularly light and free. She is overcome by the sheer wonder of it all; a mild, satisfying intoxication numbs her sense of reality.

"I know you," she exclaims with joy as the vision remains before her, distinct and at rest. A moment later she is not so sure. "I don't know you." She utters the words with trepidation, for the vision seems restless and excited.

"Who are you? . . . . . I don't know you. . . . . Oh, that I knew!". . . . .

Then into her ears whispered words wing themselves, bringing the answer, and with the answer, repose. They are words she has heard before but up to now has failed to comprehend.

"It is Jesus."

She responds gently: "Yes . . . . it is Jesus."

In the recesses of her recently disturbed mind she now finds peace.

Naturally, her first reaction to this Jesus is purely personal. Jesus was far superior to Dumont, or Isaac Van Wagener, but nevertheless he remained in her mind a man. Her man! No one else might have him or claim him in just the way she did. "What!" she exclaims, "others know Jesus? I am the only one who *knows* Jesus!"

She approaches all persons who she thinks can bring her closer to a true understanding of this great mystery. Will they tell her all about Him? Will they read to her (since she cannot read) out of the New Testament?

Naïvely she interrupts one person who is reading to her to inquire, "Is Jesus married?"

And when, with considerable sense of consternation, her informant replies hurriedly, "What! God have a wife?" Isabella continues her probing like a surgeon unwilling to lay down the scalpel until the issue is settled, and asks, "Is Jesus God?"

However, although she is told over and over that Jesus and God are synonymous, or at least that some Christians so believe, she will not have it so. She never comprehended it that way. If Jesus was God, how could he stand between God and her? A reasonable enough question! Assuredly, he was not God. Rather, he was a friend, who interceded for her to God, and through whom love flowed back and forth from God to her, as from a fountain. That was why she loved everybody now. No one could make her hate him. She even forgot her hatred of John Nealy, and Mrs. Dumont; of white folk in general, even though they still placed chains around her people.

From this time, so much love flowed through her heart that evermore she will be concerned primarily with one single reason for living: to let the love of God work miracles in the hearts of men, even her enemies, so that men and women everywhere, of every race and class, may be united and free. And for such love she will forsake even peace—yea, for such love she will rebel and even fight.

§ 7

Isabella's God was a jealous God.

Even though she had drawn close to Him, she had been too late to escape the retribution for gross neglect. She will learn that there is no such thing on earth as individual freedom; that the acts of one person must always be considered in the light of their effects on others.

When she had left Dumont, she had separated herself from her children as well as from her husband. One of them, Peter, a boy of five years, was in special need of a mother's supervision and care. Because there was little more than a year for slavery to continue in New York State, she probably assumed that no substantial changes would be made on the Dumont estate during that time; and even if Dumont sold any of her children, he would have to confine his sale within the borders of the state, for the law expressly forbade sales of slaves across state lines. In all probability, therefore, Peter and her other children would be kept sufficiently close to her to enable her to keep a watchful eye even though at a distance. But her chief reliance was on Dumont, who she was sure would never permit any of her children to be sold away.

She should have known better. Masters are inevitably self-interested. Both Dumont and the law failed her.

Her former master did sell her five-year-old Peter to a certain Dr. Gedney, whose intention was to take him as a kind of valet on a trip to England. The understanding was that the boy should be returned to New York in time to be emancipated under the law; but this, of course, was pure risk.

Peter, however, proved to be too young to be of use to Dr. Gedney, and he was transferred to the physician's brother, Solomon Gedney, who lived near Dumont. This man in turn sold him to the husband of his sister, Eliza Gedney. He, a wealthy Alabama planter named Fowler, in defiance of the law of New York State, took the boy back with him to Alabama.

Isabella was horrified when she learned about the fate of her son. She was to learn, however, that God is no respecter of shocked feelings. Here, now, was a nice turn of events. Behold how her own self-achieved emancipation had only made it easier for this worst kind of enslavement to fasten itself upon her boy.

There was but one remedy.

Without a moment's hesitation, Isabella set out, barefooted and stockingless, to reclaim her lost boy.

Picture this Negro woman. She is free, but in appearance she is not unlike many another slave. Clad in a queer cotton dress, with a large colored handkerchief over her head; her gait awkward, what with the upward thrust of her trunk and the forward drive of her right leg; as she trots over the sandy road in her stockingless, bare feet, she seems like the last creature in the world to battle against an entire class of society, yea, against the very state, in order to reclaim for herself the boy who has been sent so far away from her. But this woman dares to do just that.

When she arrives at New Paltz, she hastens to the Dumont estate to register bitter complaint about her former master's treatment of her boy.

Mrs. Dumont overheard her remonstrances.

"Ugh," she exclaimed, "a fine furor to make about a little nigger! Why, haven't you as many of them left as you can see to take care of? A pity 'tis the niggers are not all in Guinea! Making such a hulla-baloo over the neighborhood; and all for a paltry nigger!"

Isabella listened quietly to this heartless talk. Little as she feared the woman, she respected her even less. She hesitated a moment before answering, for experience was bestowing poise upon her, and past victories over trying problems were adding the gentle assurance which later is implicit in her queenly bearing and her sometimes imperious repartee.

With a gentle sense of determination which by its very calmness must have infuriated her former mistress, she replied, simply, "I'll have my child again."

"Have your child again!" Mrs. Dumont's voice was filled with contempt and scorn. "You? How can you get him? And what have you to support him with even if you had him? Have you any money?"

"No," Isabella replied, with the same quiet but marked emphasis, "I have no money..... But God has enough— or what is better than money..... And I'll have my child again."

Isabella was not merely uttering words. Neither was she expressing simply a conviction or a hope. She could not have felt differently or have expressed herself differently if she had desired. She felt the "power of the Lord" descending upon her, penetrating every pore of her body, and issuing from her again like a rush of mighty voices from under a covering sheath. This power ex-

panded within her and surged upward. She did not need
to look up to the heavens for strength or confidence; she
herself was towering towards the stars, and heaven was
coming down to meet her. She could say later, "I felt *so
tall* within. I felt as if the power of a nation was with me."

The power of a nation. She had been her own emanci-
pator; few had known about that experience. Now she
would emancipate her son, and the countryside would
applaud. Later, through civil war, all her kinsmen would
be freed, and the nation and the world would echo with
eternal praises.

"I'll have my child again."

She was on the *Lord's* side. No need to lose time arguing
with an unspiritual creature like Mrs. Dumont. It would
be well to let *Him* deal with the likes of her.

Perhaps, though, Mrs. Gedney, Eliza Gedney's mother,
would lend some aid. It would do no harm to find out.

Mrs. Gedney met Isabella at the front door. Half amused,
half disdainful, she listened while the ex-slave poured out
to her the deep distress which was in her heart. Then, when
in grief and indignation she cried out, "I will have him back
again," the unsympathetic mother-in-law of Peter's ab-
ductor saw fit to react with the utmost nonchalance.

"Dear me!" she said, speaking at first with a conde-
scending superciliousness, "what a disturbance to make
about your child!" Then, with evident disdain, "What!
Is your child better than *my* child? My child is gone out
there, and yours is gone to live with her, to have enough
of everything, and to be treated like a gentleman."

She mocked and laughed at Isabella's absurd indignation.

"Your child," Isabella continued, "has gone there, but
she is married, and my boy has gone as a slave. He is too
little to go so far from his mother."

She felt her heart breaking.

"Oh, I must have my child!" she sobbed.

Not an atom of sympathy from Mrs. Gedney. She laughed more demoniacally.

No need to have come here either. Isabella took her leave, feeling by this time dejected and quite alone.

But yes! These are the proper times to call upon Jehovah. She prayed fervently.

"Oh, God," she exclaimed, directly still but with the simplicity now of reverence, "show these people. Show this woman. Show them all that you are my helper."

With her accustomed resourcefulness, however, she left no stone unturned in assisting God to assist her.

It was very unusual to hear of a slave's making so much clamor over the sale of a child. True, Isabella was no longer a bondswoman, but even then she must realize that Peter, her son, did not legally belong to her. Has she forgotten completely the slave code to which she had subscribed so heartily all those years she was with Dumont? What was this new freedom which had got into her bones? No wonder Mrs. Dumont scorned her, and Mrs. Gedney laughed. Crazy woman! To make so much to-do over a nigger brat! A tempest in a teapot!

But the tempest flew out of the pot. People all around New Paltz began talking about this black woman who let no one have any peace about her lost boy. One day a man approached her and expressed the deepest sympathy. He even gave her advice.

"Why don't you go to the Quakers?" he advised her. "They feel a great concern about your boy. They are indignant. I am sure they will help you."

He pointed out to her two houses where Quakers dwelt.

"Go there," he counselled. "They will surely help you."

At one of these houses she poured out her tale of woe. It was evening. Her friends listened sympathetically, fed her, and gave her a room for the night. Timid still, despite her experiences at the Van Wagener home, she found it hard again to sleep in the clear white, beautiful bed to which they directed her. For a long while she debated whether she should sleep in it or lie underneath it on the floor. This time she made a compromise. She did sleep on the floor, but before daybreak she entered the bed, in order to spare offense to her benefactors.

Taking Dumont, or his wife, or even God to task, were matters as simple as breathing. These were royal prerogatives. But somehow she could not get used to believing that she was one of these so-called ladies!

In the morning, the Quaker friends sent her to Kingston where the Grand Jury was in session. There she could go to the courthouse and enter a complaint about her boy. When she had arrived at the courthouse, she stood and looked at it for a moment before entering. After she had passed through the door, she asked the first imposing person she saw where the Grand Jury was. Before he could direct her, she had unfolded her story to him. She had the idea that anyone would want to hear such a harrowing tale. This man listened with a cold, detached air, then merely instructed her to go upstairs.

The congestion on the stairway was so great that she had great difficulty reaching the next floor. She looked around again for an important-looking person, then rushed to the first one she saw, exclaiming, "Sir, be you a grand jury?"

The man looked at this curious black creature, standing there before him in her plain cotton dress, the inevitable kerchief around her head, her feet still stockingless and shoeless, and those expressive eyes of hers so big with the wonder of a totally new experience. He must have been highly amused both at her appearance and her question.

"Why do you ask that?" he inquired of her.

"I want to find out about my son," she replied, and proceeded once more to relate her story.

This man, however, listened until she had finished. Then, pointing to a room, he said to her, "You go in there; there is where the Grand Jury sits."

She found the "grand jurors" sitting by a table. A certain Lawyer Chip, a member of the jury, arose and led her into his office. He asked her what her mission was, and when she had finished her story he said to her, "Can you swear that the child you speak of is your son?"

"Yes," Isabella replied, "I swear it is my son."

"Stop, stop," shouted Chip, who believed in adhering to formalities, "you must swear by this book."

Isabella reached for the proffered Bible and, placing it to her lips, began to mumble over it, "I swear it is my son."

Some clerks who were in the room were overcome with merriment at seeing this barefooted Negro woman kissing a Bible and swearing in this fashion. They burst out into boisterous laughter.

"What good is it," asked one of them, "to make *her* swear?"

"It will answer the law," Chip replied.

The lawyer gave her a writ and told her to take it to the constable of New Paltz in order that he might serve it on Solomon Gedney.

Now she was getting somewhere.

But it was nearly ten miles to New Paltz, and Isabella had to walk the entire distance. Alas, the constable there made a fatal mistake for, instead of serving the writ on Solomon Gedney, he served it on the man's brother. This gave Solomon an opportunity to learn about the writ, and he took advantage of the respite to slip into a near-by boat and sail across the North River. A short while later, Isabella and the constable discovered their mistake, but all they could do was look on helplessly from the shore while the accused man fled across the river. Upon the lawyer's advice, Solomon went to Alabama in order to get the boy and avoid imprisonment and a large fine.

It was in the spring, months later, that he returned with the child. He was confident that the matter would be dropped from this point, because in New York State he was legally entitled to the boy. But the tiger in Isabella had been unleashed. She would not be satisfied now until her child's freedom had been achieved.

Upon Lawyer Chip's advice, the original warrant was served. Lo! Solomon Gedney, slaveowner, not only was arrested and taken to Kingston at the behest of a black woman and a former slave, but he was made to post six hundred dollars for appearance in court.

What have Mrs. Dumont and Mrs. Gedney to say now? They would know that Isabella's God was a mighty God!

Here, however, the case encountered another snag. American court procedure was as long drawn out in 1826 as it is to-day.

"Your case must lie over till the next session of the court," her lawyer instructed her. "That will not be for some months. . . . . The law must take its course."

"What," agonized Isabella, "wait another court! Wait months? Why, long before that time Gedney can clear off and take my child with him no one knows where. I cannot wait. I must have him now, while he is to be had."

Lawyer Chip's patience was about at an end. What was the matter with this Negro woman? Had he not done more for her already than he usually attempted to do for a dozen Negroes? Yet here she was at every turn of the road, insisting upon further concessions.

"Well," he answered rather icily, "If Gedney puts the boy out of the way, he must pay the six hundred dollars, and one half of this will be yours."

This mercenary attitude aroused an indignant protest in Isabella.

"I am not interested in the money," she answered. "I

want only my son. I want him. I must have him, and I must have him right away."

"You are being unreasonable," retorted Lawyer Chip. "You ought to be very thankful for all that has been done for you. You have had a great deal accomplished already. There is nothing left for you to do but wait patiently for the court to reopen."

Words like these had no effect on the irrepressible Isabella. She knew now where her lawyer was—but where was God?

"Oh, Lord," she implored, "give my son into my hands, and that right away! Don't let the spoilers have him any longer!"

And now, because she was sure that everyone was tired of her petitions—Chip, the Quakers, and even God—she resorted to the newly found Jesus. If he was the great intercessor, now more than ever was his great opportunity to prove his effectiveness. This was to be the supreme test. Let Jesus show the way.

She prayed to Jesus.

She walked about almost aimlessly. One moment she was calling out to Jesus to intercede for her before the throne of the Almighty; the next moment she was assailed with doubts and crying out in her anguish, "Who will show me any good, and lend a helping hand in this matter?"

When a perfect stranger accosted her on the street, she knew that Jesus had heard her prayer.

"Hello, there," he said, "how are you getting along with your boy? Are they giving him up to you?"

"No," the astonished woman replied. Eagerly, once more, she poured out her story to this new volunteer friend. In mournful tones she admitted that she had tried the patience of her benefactors; that nobody would help her further.

"Look here," the stranger exclaimed, "I tell you what you had better do. Do you see that stone house yonder?"

He pointed out a building to her. Isabella nodded.

"Well, Lawyer Demain lives there. You go to him and lay your case before him. I think he'll help you. Stick to him. Don't give him peace until he does help you. I feel sure if you press him, he'll do it for you."

Isabella needed no further bidding. She trotted off in her bare feet to the lawyer's house.

Lawyer Demain, after receiving her politely, listened to the story which in all probability he had heard many persons discuss previously. Isabella's unique personality and her appearance intrigued him. He sat silent a few minutes, simply looking at her. Then he said, "For five dollars I will get your son within twenty-four hours."

Only five dollars!

"Money!" thought Isabella, who had never had a dollar in her life. "Why, I have no money!" she exclaimed.

"Go back to your Quaker friends who carried you to the court," the lawyer said. "They certainly will help you to get five dollars. I have no doubt about that. And you shall have your son within twenty-four hours from the time you bring me that amount."

On foot she traveled back to her Quaker friends who lived in a section known as Poppletown. These people were glad to let her have funds. She received nearly twenty dollars, and rushed back to New Paltz carrying the money tightly in her hands.

Some friends heard about the additional money and asked her what she was doing with it.

"Oh," she replied, "I got it for Lawyer Demain, and I gave it to him."

"But why didn't you purchase shoes and other things you need with the remainder of the money?" they inquired of her.

"I don't want money or clothes now," she said to them.

"I want only my son. If five dollars will get him, twenty dollars will surely get him."

She remembered the stranger's advice, and clung so close to Lawyer Demain that the lawyer must have decided that he had not made a very good bargain after all. Although he had arranged for her to remain at the home of Mr. Rutzer, a friend, until he had procured the child, each hour or so Isabella called at his office or his home in order to find out whether or not Peter had been returned. It became so annoying that the lawyer's servant had to warn him of Isabella's presence at the front door.

She knew that she was wearing thin her welcome. But how could she help herself? She must see her boy, and every minute seemed like eternity. Even the repeated assurances of Lawyer Demain that she should have Peter on the following morning did not satisfy her.

"I said within twenty-four hours," he reminded her, after one of her frequent inquiries. "I have until some time tomorrow to produce the boy. You must give me until then."

Still not altogether reassured, Isabella departed for the day; but the next morning she returned before the lawyer was out of bed.

Petulantly the lawyer rebuked her.

"I have told you over and over that you will have the boy to-day," he said. "You must be patient. I have until noon. I have already sent Matty Styles after him. He is the best constable around here. He will surely come back with your boy and his master, either dead or alive. You will surely see your son again. But," he added wearily, "do not come here again until I send for you. I will let you know when he has arrived."

A few hours later, Lawyer Demain came for her.

"Your boy is here," he informed the overjoyed woman.

"But," he added, "he stoutly denies having any mother or
other relative over at Dumont's. You will have to go over
and identify him."

It did not take a moment to hasten to the office where
the boy was being held. They opened the door. There
was her boy. Isabella rushed over to greet him, but on seeing his mother he cried out in terrible alarm, and, kneeling
before his master, pleaded with all the people in the room
not to let him be taken from Gedney.

"Please don't let her take me from my master!" the boy
screamed, with the tears running down his cheeks. "He
has been so good to me. He brought me all the way up
from the South."

His tearful eyes looked at Isabella as if he thought she
was an ogre about to seize and maul him to death.

There were some very noticeable scars on his face, and
some one asked him, "Where did you get that scar on your
forehead?"

"Fowler's horse hove me," he replied.

"And in your cheek?"

"I did that running against the carriage."

The Justice in the case noticed, however, that each time
the boy began to answer a question he would look up at
Gedney as if, instead of being terrified at Isabella's presence, he really was afraid that he might give the wrong
answer to the question and thereby incriminate his master.
He assured the boy that he had nothing to fear from the
persons in the room, and urged him to forget that his
master was there; all he was to do was to answer the question which was being asked as truthfully as he knew how.
Nevertheless, the boy persisted in his plea to remain with
Gedney, and swore that Isabella was not his mother.

There must have been enough resemblance between the
two to dispel all doubt; because when Lawyer Demain
argued that the boy should be given over into the custody
of Isabella on her claiming to be its mother, the Justice

agreed, declaring that the child "should be delivered into the hands of the mother, having no other master, no other controller, no other conductor, but his mother." Thereupon he deprived Gedney of any other claim to the lad, and turned him over to Isabella.

Still the child whimpered and moaned, in terror lest Gedney pursue and assault him. It took a long time to assure him that Gedney could do nothing to him. After a while he was convinced. He became quite calm, and then he said to Isabella, as if he were awaking from a horrible nightmare, "You *do* look like my mother used to."

Now he told a different story.

When Isabella examined him to see if there were further bruises, she discovered that from head to foot he was a welter of black marks and hard places, showing where he had suffered mistreatment.

"Heavens!" she exclaimed, running her hands over some of the injuries, "what is all this?"

"It is where Fowler whipped me," the boy replied.

"And this?"

"Where he kicked me."

"And this?"

"Where he beat me."

"O Lord Jesus," Isabella cried, "look! See my poor child."

Suddenly she was overcome with bitterness. Succumbing to the storm of a mighty vindictive reaction, she exclaimed, "O Lord, render unto them double for all this!"

Then turning to her boy she moaned, "O my God, Pete, how did you bear it?"

"Oh, this is nothing, mammy," said Pete lightly, now that he had thoroughly warmed up to the new status of affairs, "you should see Phillis. I guess you *would* be scared then. She had a little baby too, but Fowler cut her till the milk and blood ran down her body. You would certainly scare to see Phillis, mammy."

"Well," Isabella inquired, "what did Miss Fowler say, Pete, when you were treated so badly."

"Oh, mammy, she said she wished I was with you. Sometimes, mammy, I would crawl under the stoop with the blood running all around me. My back would stick to the boards. And sometimes Mrs. Eliza would wait until everyone was asleep and come to grease my sores."

Isabella sobbed bitterly.

"Poor, poor child," she cried.

Isabella's God was a vengeful God.

Lo! a short time later, did not the same Fowler brutally murder Eliza Gedney, his wife? According to the report which Isabella received, Eliza Fowler's mother, the same Mrs. Gedney who scoffed at her own distraction because of the sale of Peter, went completely insane, walking about deliriously and calling out repeatedly, "Eliza! Eliza!"

Isabella recalled her vindictive plea to Jehovah. How ghastly this development appeared to her! Now that her child had been restored to her safe and nearly whole, she had no need for further retribution, divine or otherwise. It was all a horrible nightmare. She murmured to God in her astonishment at this devastating aftermath of indignant prayer, whispering to Him as a little child might whisper to a parent.

"That's too much, God," she confided to Him. "That's too much. I did not mean quite so much."

Terrible. Terrible. But it was God's way; and His way was her way. He established the laws for both slave and master. She had better let God settle His affairs as He wished.

The year 1827 has come and gone.

The saga of servitude has ended. For Isabella and for her children had been the stripes and the bruises, but now, in the state of New York at least, they were all free. Masters and mistresses would have their time of it along with the sorry blacks.

Isabella was tired of the whole association. She had known nothing but serfdom and the villainy of masters against their slaves. Enough now of these villages and their slave notions! New York City, the metropolis, that was the place. Life would be exciting enough there and to spare. She would meet all kinds of people and ideas. She'd get a chance to expand. Living would not be a concern, for there was no dearth of work in the great port.

She had her son placed under careful supervision in a town called Wahkendall. Then she visited about a little, seeing among others a sister Sophia at Newburgh whom she had lost for seventeen years. It was time now to pack up her belongings, take up her baby girl, and add her individuality to that unending stream which already was making the gateway of the East the metropolis of the world.

II

Matthias

WHEN ISABELLA ARRIVED in New York City about the year 1829, one of the first things she did after obtaining employment was to join the church. At first she attended the class for Negroes in a Methodist church on John Street, but later she transferred to the Zion African Church on Church Street.

Here a very strange thing happened.

During one of the services, she walked to the altar in the front of the church, and there, while kneeling in prayer, she extended her hand to another woman who prayed beside her. For no reason that she could comprehend she gave a start when she grasped the woman's hand. There was something strikingly strange and yet familiar about that person whose handclasp symbolized the "speaking promise" of spiritual kinship.

That the hand of a woman should be bony and hard ought not to seem queer when its possessor was a Negro, but nevertheless Isabella was shocked by the mere touch. She looked up into the other woman's face. That face seemed curiously familiar also. It bore a resemblance to someone she had known very intimately.

Where, where have I seen you before, she mused to herself. She searched her mind but the answer was not there. Over and over she conjured up the woman's image, striving desperately to re-establish the bond that would bring back the association which she was confident once existed between them. But it was no use; she always just missed forming the connection. Days passed, and eventually the memory of the woman grew dim.

A while later, Isabella's sister Sophia also came to New York City to live. She sought out Isabella, who had difficulty in recognizing her in her resplendent garments.

They felicitated each other on the renewal of their lives together, and then Sophia said, "I have another surprise for you."

"And what is this surprise?" asked Isabella, not entirely recovered from the shock of her sister's visit.

"Your brother Michel is in the city."

"Michel!" Isabella gasped. She could not believe her ears. "You don't mean the one that Mau-Mau used to tell us about in the sleigh?"

"That very one," her sister replied, and she took Isabella with her to find him.

When they reached Michel, his joy over meeting Isabella whom he had never seen before was softened by distressing news which he had to impart to his sisters.

"If only you had come a little sooner," he said to Isabella.

"Why?" she asked.

"Then you would have met Nancy also, your sister who was shut up with me in the sleigh."

"Why, where is Nancy?" inquired Isabella.

"Dead," was her brother's response. "She died just a few months ago."

While the three commiserated together and bemoaned the lost sister, Michel imparted bits of information regarding Nancy. He described her manner, her dress, her appearance in general. Then he added that she formerly attended Zion Church.

"Lord God have mercy!" thought Isabella.

"Why," she said, "she's the woman I've been trying to remember ever since we made the 'speaking promise' at the altar. Thank God, I did see her. That was Nancy. I have seen my sister Nancy; and it was Mau-Mau's picture written all over her face that made me know her."

The two sisters and brother wept together silently.

Isabella's deep religious devotion was not long in attracting attention. In the three or four years since her religious conversion, she probably had advanced in power in the church. She prayed extremely well, which is to say that she could talk easily with her God. She could pray to practically any length, and with her praying she was able to stir an audience to unusual heights. She believed she had witnessed responses to so many of her prayers that her utterances contained the deep conviction which few persons since the disciples of Jesus could muster.

While she probably knew no formal music (unauthentic reports state that she played the bass violin), she managed her emotional notes with a virtuosity which amounted to genius. She was mistress of pathos and humor, and she possessed a direct petitioning manner which carried her and her hearers far up into the realms of a living heaven.

She was by nature forceful, of rapid-fire mentality, original, unique. Her voice, too, just suited her manner. It was so low that if you had not seen her you would have thought it belonged to a man; but it was not in the least unpleasant. Usually she spoke in a very quiet tone, but when occasion demanded she could shout until the very gates of heaven seemed ready to open at her command. Besides, she could sing. Her fervent voice, leading in the old Methodist hymns, was sure to be heard at every service she attended.

Whether or not she had up to this time attempted to preach we have no knowledge. What attempts at preaching she may have made must have been of the most experimental nature. She had not yet enjoyed active experience in organized church work to make her sure in the various types of religious leadership. Besides, she suffered the handicap of not being able to read. She never will be able to read a line, not even of the Bible, so that when later she plays upon the hearts of her listeners with sermons composed out of the whole cloth of her remarkably full life, she will always use as a theme one subject, and only one— the subject which represented the experience above all others in her life which shone like a transcendent sun— "When I found Jesus."

One of the first persons in New York City to be attracted by her flair for religious expression was a certain Mr. Latourette, with whom she lived for a time as a house servant. He was a very emotional, deeply religious man, and a member of an almost fanatically religious group that was experimenting at this time with various forms of religious practices. For it should be recalled that the period of the early 1830's, in some respects not unlike the 1930's, was one of extreme religious attitudes throughout the eastern part of the United States.

This employer assumes little importance in Isabella's life, but it was through him that she met a person who was to become a great influence in the next few years of her residence in the metropolis. This man's name was Elijah Pierson. He was a well-to-do merchant, and he and his story deserve more than passing comment in any life of this woman.

Unquestionably Elijah Pierson was an unbalanced religious devotee. Originally a member of the Presbyterian Church, he had, in 1822, severed his connection with that body, and affiliated with the Baptist denomination. Here, for a number of years, he gained the reputation of being a sincere, quiet, devoted Christian gentleman.

His wife Sarah was a perfect complement. Small, graceful, intelligent and intellectually inclined, she became one of the most interesting and beloved individuals in her circle. She, too, had left the denomination of her original choice, in her case the Episcopal Church, to go over with her husband to the Baptists. Like her husband, too, she was very keenly interested in humanitarian problems, and was susceptible to any suggestion which promised to benefit large masses of people.

Some time prior to 1828, when the religious fervor of numerous groups in New York City was being manifested by an almost infinite succession of prayer meetings, these two persons received an urge to revive religion among all the people in the metropolis. They reasoned that after everyone in New York City had been converted, the whole world would see the blaze that had fired the city and turn towards God. Missionaries could then be sent to Europe to complete the program of world conversion.

Now Pierson began to pray incessantly, and to spend whole days in fasting, abstaining from water as well as bread. Later, under Pierson's influence, Isabella attempts the same practices.

The man and wife became particularly outspoken in denunciation of pew-renting, among other things; then gradually other differences with the Baptist Church developed. For a while they bore themselves with the calm dignity which befitted their station, but it was becoming noticeable that their religious attitude was verging more and more on that of deranged people.

They were particularly interested in the plight of fallen women. It may have been in one of the institutions for such persons (the Magdalene House mentioned below) that Isabella first made the acquaintance of Pierson, for she, too, had become interested in these types. What he and his wife felt about their duty towards these fallen creatures may be noted from a page out of the daily book which the two of them wrote together:

Prayer for the harlots of Five Points: Asked the Lord to give us all the ground whereupon the soles of our feet had trod, and all the souls now alive who had heard our voices in the neighborhood.

Answer: The Lord said, "You must go and fetch them out." The Lord said, concerning the two witnesses, "Thou art one and Sarah the other."

By 1829, the differences of the Piersons with the Baptist Church had grown so wide that it became necessary to leave the church completely. Thereupon they dispensed with their elegant housefurnishings, moved down to the Bowery, and there opened their home to people who had religious feelings similar to their own. Disciples flocked to the strange group with their curious slants on the Bible and on God. Soon a thriving sect was established.

While we cannot be certain, it seems reasonable to believe that Isabella attended some of these meetings. In all probability she had met Pierson by this time, and her early impressions of the man were of such a nature that without doubt she would have responded to his invitation to meet with his group. It was about this time, too, that the Piersons had become interested in the Magdalene House, a refuge for girls. Through the intercession of Mr. Latourette, Isabella had been sent to this hospice in order to help with the religious work carried on there; it is altogether likely that it was in this place that she and Elijah Pierson met.

Pierson became a preacher, but when the Baptist Church refused to give him a license, he continued independently. Now he and his wife decided that they would establish "the kingdom" about which they had been talking for a long time. That kingdom should be located right on Bowery Hill! Established it was in Mr. Pierson's house on Bowery Hill.

Some persons have attempted to attach Isabella to this original "kingdom," but according to her own testimony, and from other evidence, we are led to believe that, if she attended any of the meetings held there, it was merely as a casual visitor.

Religious fervor in the "kingdom" developed fast and furiously. Sometimes these gatherings continued for two or three weeks, with as many as fourteen meetings held in a single week. Interspersed would be prayer and fasting. Usually, the only time taken out was a few hours for sleep or slight refreshment. Was it from these meetings that Isabella learned to fast? She had observed Elijah Pierson during his own periods of fasting, which lasted usually two nights and a day, and inquired of him its real purpose.

"Fasting gives light inwardly and spiritually," he had informed her.

She mused to herself in that inimitable manner of hers.

"If fasting will do that, I'll fast too, for I need light as much as anybody."

But she outstripped Pierson, and fasted three whole days and nights, not even taking a drop of water. On the fourth day she started to the pantry and fell to the floor. She picked herself up finally, but for fear that she would offend the Almighty she consumed only dry bread and water.

She mused more.

"Surely I've got light," she said to herself, "but it is all in the body and none in my mind! I feel so light, and so well . . . . . I could skim around like a gull!"

But we believe this experience occurred a year or so later than those of the early days of Pierson's kingdom.

Thus, under the tutelage of the Piersons, there developed a church, the Five Points House, an ascetic group called the "Retrenchment Society," and the Magdalene Asylum, where Isabella assisted in the religious services. Meanwhile, Elijah Pierson, owing to his fasting habits, became only a shadow of his former self, and his wife's body gave way completely. In the winter of 1830 her health declined so greatly that by the spring practically all hope of recovery had been abandoned.

But Elijah Pierson believed that somehow God would bring recovery to his wife. Day by day he continued praying and fasting, holding steadily to the belief that his wife would be restored. As late as June, 1830, he wrote in his diary, "Day of fasting and prayer for Sarah. It seemed the Lord said, 'Sarah thy wife shall recover.'"

We must pause to note the entry of June 20, 1830, for it will have a signal influence on certain future actions of Isabella. The entry reads:

"I have named thee this day Elijah the Tishbite, and thou shalt go before me in the spirit of power of Elias, to prepare my way for me."

On the very next day, as Pierson was riding in an omnibus on Wall Street, he imagined he heard God speaking to him, saying, "Thou art Elijah the Tishbite. Gather unto me all the members of Israel at the foot of Mount Carmel."

Pierson understood by this that he must convene the leading members of his church at his house on Bowery Hill. For was not his church Israel, and her elders the members? Not long after, these members, of whom Isabella probably was one though we cannot be absolutely certain, came and seated themselves around the bedside of Mrs. Pierson. Their curiosity about this sudden summons was soon satisfied, for Pierson announced that it was his intention to anoint his wife in order that her cure might be effected according to St. James, who had written, "Is any among you sick? Let him call for the elders of the church, and let them pray over him, anointing him with oil, in the name of the Lord. And the prayer of faith shall save the sick, and the Lord shall raise him up."

Whether or not Isabella was present and active in this service, as one witness contends, is a matter of conjecture. It really does not matter. That her name should be brought up in this connection indicates to what extent she had brought recognition to herself as an important religious figure. What we need not doubt is that Isabella was suffi-

ciently conditioned, emotionally, by this time, to carry on
with such a service.

However, the much-heralded cure did not materialize.
Instead, Mrs. Pierson's strength declined rapidly, and a
short while afterwards she died. Then ensued a queer
development which is only the beginning of queer happenings which do not conclude until the great city is convulsed at the amazing religious aberrations of the Pierson
cult, and Isabella's name becomes a byword on the lips of
thousands of incredulous fellow-citizens.

Elijah Pierson declared to his flock that the last service
for his wife should not be a funeral, but instead it was to
be a resurrection!

As far as he was able, he was as good as his word. He
took an open Bible in his hand, then entered the room
where the body of his wife lay and reread the passage
from St. James which had proved ineffectual in preserving
her life.

Now he uttered a prayer which must have rejoiced the
heart of the Negro woman if she was present, because she
was of all things a praying soul.

"O Lord God of Israel," he prayed, "thy own word de-
clares that if the elders of the church anoint the sick and
pray over him, the Lord shall raise him up. We have taken
thee at thy word; we have anointed her with oil, and prayed
the prayer of faith, and thou knowest in this faith the
dead woman died, and in this faith we thy children live.

"Now, Lord, we claim thy promise. God is not man that
he should die, and if this dear woman is not raised up this
day, thy word will fall to the ground; thy promise is null
and void.... Thou knowest we have performed the
condition to the very letter. O Lord, now fulfill thy
promise!"

What must have been the emotions which passed
through the heart of Isabella if, as is more than probable,

she was present at this remarkable ceremony! What would not anyone give to have seen those lustrous eyes, wide and round like moons, full of the most childlike faith, and lighted with the expectancy of a child who does not doubt that the father will grant her petition!

But of course nothing happened.

The throng of people gathered there waited until another preacher arose, and, in order to save face for Pierson, announced that Sarah Pierson would rise again in the great Judgment Day.

This may not have satisfied every person assembled at the disappointing ceremony. Future events indicate that it was a satisfactory interpretation for Pierson. It was satisfactory for Isabella, too.

In connection with the life of Isabella, none of these events would be of more than passing interest were it not for the fact that they were leading up to important happenings which would involve both Isabella and Elijah Pierson. At some time between 1829 and 1832, Isabella became a servant in the Pierson home. A strong religious attachment developed between employer and servant. They shared their religious experiences, and Isabella became devoted on principle to the man who seemed such a sincere believer in the Christian mysteries.

Her life with Pierson only increased her desire to serve Jehovah in every way possible. Everything her employer said to her impressed her as being gospel truth. We have already referred to her experiments with fasting. A man like Pierson would have many queer ideas relative to the Bible and to Christian experience. His actions during the illness of his wife were quite characteristic of his fanatical frame of mind. Isabella acquired these ideas by association.

Two ideas more than any others were his constant obsession. One of these was that in some way he would meet his wife again on this earth, possibly in some reincar-

nated form, and the other, that he would be used by God
to establish the kingdom of heaven on earth. Consequently
he was the prey and dupe of any individual or cult whose
teachings showed promise of bringing these things to pass.

Naturally, he talked about these things both within and
without his intimate circle. Isabella must have heard no end
of discussion about the new day when he should play the
rôle of Elijah according to the call that had come down
upon him in the omnibus. She knew of his longings to be
with his wife once more, and of his passionate desire to be
instrumental in saving the world.

As a result, Isabella was as much a believer in these
auguries as he was. You could trust her vivid imagination
for that. But, also, it must be remembered that she had
sufficient reason from her own experience for believing
that her God not only could but did perform wondrous
deeds. Now that she was with this pious man, who treated
her with every courtesy, who interpreted the Scriptures
for her and painfully instructed her in prophecy, it would
have been very strange had she not reacted with a stirring
conviction that something like the millennium was near at
hand.

It was in the air, almost everywhere in the country. Isabella merely happened to be in a place where some of these
beliefs were accepted even more literally than many people
found necessary. Consequently, she was ready for any
development; indeed she was eager to be present in the
place and on the day when these great things happened.

The day is approaching when she will get her wish, or
so she will imagine; for, just about this time there come
rumors of one who is claiming to be a prophet from on
high, by name Matthias. He is now on his way to the great
city preparatory to saving the world. He will not be long
making Isabella's acquaintance, and that believer's mind,
prepared for just such an individual as he will claim to be,
will leap to his coming as a hound leaps for a fox. She will

relay the news to her benefactor, Pierson, who immediately
will conclude that his hopes are about to be realized. Then
a strange drama will begin, involving Pierson, a wealthy
friend of Pierson's named Mills, Isabella, and several others.

But now a word about Matthias.

It appears that at the same time that the Piersons were
beginning to have their troubles with the Baptist Church,
this man Matthias was having similar experiences in another part of New York State.

Robert Matthews, or Matthias as he called himself later,
had been born in the state, and had grown up in the Presbyterian faith. When he was a little child, a minister placed
his hand on his head and pronounced a blessing. From that
moment Robert Matthews was certain that he would become a famous person. From that moment, too, Elijah
Pierson and Isabella were foreordained to incomparable
religious vicissitudes.

Up to his eighteenth year, Matthews had engaged in
farming. Then he turned carpenter. About 1813, he married and wandered to Cambridge, Massachusetts. Here he
met with business reverses, and about 1816 he returned to
Albany, where he attended the Dutch Reformed Church.
His excitement over religious matters was noted, especially
when the question involved temperance or the use of meats.
Gradually these fixations affected his work, until no one
would employ him.

By 1829, as a result of frequent discussion and exhorta-
tion on street corners, he had gained considerable local
renown. In 1830 he expanded this somewhat dubious fame
by prophesying that Albany would be destroyed together
with its inhabitants.

Shortly after this he had a vision. He was preparing to
attend the installation of a minister at his church and,
being quite dexterous where the Bible was concerned, sat
down before a table to shave himself and read from the

Bible at the same time. While he was getting the soap ready, his eyes glimpsed a passage of Scripture which caused him to leap from his chair exclaiming, "I have found it—I have found a text which proves that no man who shaves his beard can be a true Christian."

Thereupon he attended the installation service unkempt and with unshaven beard. Towards the end of the ceremony he asked permission to ascend the pulpit and address the congregation. After hurling at his listeners a dozen or more threats purporting to issue from the Almighty, he could only be brought down from the pulpit through the expedient of extinguishing the lights.

After this, Matthews went about town haranguing any who would listen to him. Finally he aroused his wife and children in the middle of the night and urged them to flee with him from the destruction which was due to overcome Albany on the following day. His wife refused to accompany him, but he ran off with three small children, traveling with them on foot for twenty-four hours without stopping. He was now at a small place called Argyle, forty miles away and, arriving far into the night at the home of a sister who dwelt there, he made a good job of terrifying her and her family by his precipitate visit.

He was forcibly ejected from the town on the next day, when he attempted to interrupt a sermon which was being preached in the village church. We find him again in Albany, making progress in a downhill sort of way. His beard was becoming more formidable in appearance daily; he took no care of his clothing, and preferred to look as grotesque as possible, for this attracted attention to him and his violent declamations about heaven, hell, and damnation.

But now he had become a public nuisance, and he was arrested repeatedly for disturbing the peace. On more than one occasion he was detained on suspicion of being a lunatic, but he never failed to prove that he was sane. However, he decided that it was too confining to remain in one place, and so he set out to travel over the country, converting sinners, and hastening the great day of judgment.

Daily he became more boisterous; daily he became more savage in appearance. He did any ridiculous thing to attract attention, then hurled vile curses at all those who scoffed or snickered. He deceived a few, however, for Old Testament quotations poured out of him like a gushing stream and, although he could make the most sublime passage of Scripture a confused and incoherent jumble of words, he had wit and wisdom enough to say some things and answer some questions in such a way as to create the illusion of an oracle.

Now he was no longer Robert Matthews, but Matthias; and he denied ever having been a Christian, but a Jew— that very Matthew of New Testament fame, merged with the Messiah. Traveling about in New York State, then down through the state of Pennsylvania, he attracted attention by the ever-increasing length of his beard, his grotesque behavior, his shabby clothes, and the old, half-starved horse which carried him about from place to place.

This was the prophet who arrived, finally, in the city of New York.

§ 2

It was inevitable that two such persons as Matthias and Pierson should meet. What would happen as a result of their first meeting would depend largely upon the nature of their immediate reactions. It may have been written in the stars that they should combine forces; this is mere conjecture. What we do know is that a catalyzing agent was at hand to effect the combination in a sure, steady process. That catalyzer was Isabella.

Matthias made the initial advance.

On May 5, 1832, he called at the home of Elijah Pierson.

That gentleman was not at home, and Isabella, who was alone in the house to receive callers, responded to Matthias' knock on the door.

Recalling the many things which Pierson had said to Isabella about the kingdom to come, it takes no lively imagination to picture her reaction when first she beheld this strange figure standing on the stoop. For presented to her was a tall man, very thin and bony but well knit together, whose thick bushy hair, with an ashy black lustre, hung profusely in huge wavy ringlets over his shoulders. It was parted in the middle, longitudinally. His sallow complexion was almost hidden beneath a long beard which grew, like the hair on his head, thick and coarse over his face, and covered his chest almost to a foot's length below the neck. On his upper lip was a thick moustache which had grown to great length and united so completely with his beard on either side that it almost concealed his mouth.

Can you see Isabella, her mouth open, her wide eyes marvelling at the wonder of the vision, leading this creature, probably walking backward before him, into the waiting room of Elijah Pierson? Her ever alert glance discerns that his walk is awkward and devoid of grace, but still there is unquestioned stateliness in his erect carriage. If this is studied effect, she has no intimation of it, because she is awed by the piercing gleam from his cold silver-gray eyes which lie sunken in their sockets like sharp piercing needle points, lighting up the pronounced features and the sallow complexion.

She is excited and decidedly not herself. Is this one of the saints of whom Pierson has spoken frequently to her? Can it be that God has sent a messenger to confirm Elijah Pierson's call? Is the "kingdom" about to be established?

As for Matthias, he is altogether self-possessed, calm, unruffled, unhurried; and as he advances slowly behind Isabella, meditating abstractedly, he seems to her to be the master of time and destiny.

Breathless and with palpitating heart, Isabella bids the stranger be seated, and watches with startled eyes to see what he will do or say. He meantime seats himself and begins immediately to discourse in long heavy sentences, interrupting himself only to meditate for a moment, or to smooth down his beard and moustache which he fondles with his long slender fingers, as one does the fur of a kitten.

Ponderously, and with an air of confidence such as only geniuses and maniacs possess, he speaks to her.

"I am Matthias," he says, "the Spirit of Truth. The Spirit of Truth disappeared from the earth at the death of Matthew in the New Testament. The Spirit of Jesus Christ entered into that Matthias, and I am the same Matthias, the apostle of the New Testament, who arose from the dead, and I possess the Spirit of Jesus of Nazareth. Jesus was God the Father, and I am God the Father, and have power to do all things; to forgive sins, to communicate the Holy Ghost to such as believe in Him."

Isabella sits or stands before him entranced, convulsed with adoration. This man! He is greater than Elijah Pierson! And had not Elijah Pierson received a direct call from heaven—been called, in fact, Elijah the Tishbite? She confides all those things which have passed between her and Pierson to the newcomer, and, overcome by the religious abstraction of the man, to say nothing of the cold severity of his countenance, she fails to observe the shrewd glance of satisfaction which spreads across Matthias' face as he drinks in every word of the valuable information.

Suddenly the prophet bursts out in stentorian tones: "All women who do not keep at home will be damned!"

"All men who wear spectacles will be damned!"

She sits in fear and trembling.

Then more quietly the voice proceeds, "From time to time God has sent his messenger on earth to enlighten mankind, from Moses to Jesus Christ, and from Jesus to

Matthias. I belong to the human race, but I have been set apart as a chosen vessel to be filled with inspiration of a lesser or greater degree, as the father directs my services. Sometimes I am ordered to speak in the first person. What the Bible has to say about the Messiah, it speaks about me and about my mission on the earth."

He pauses, meditates, cherishes his beard and moustache.

Isabella continues to gaze in wonderment. Here is glory indeed. She has talked to God far away—this is something infinitely more thrilling!

"I am a Jew."

Isabella gives a start. A Jew? But how, she wonders, in her already benumbed brain, can this great Christian be a Jew?

Matthias comprehends all that is going on in her mind. He smiles, both visibly and inwardly, and continues quietly:

"Do you not remember how Jesus prayed? 'Our Father .... who art in heaven .... thy kingdom come.....'" (shades of Mau-Mau-Bett!) "See," he cries out to the now almost hysterical woman, "it is the Father's kingdom which is to come, and not the Son's. I am He that has come to fulfill the word."

Enough. Isabella is completely overcome. The wonder of wonders has arrived. Elijah Pierson's prayer over the bier of his wife was not unavailing after all. And if Pierson is Elijah, then this person must be.....

"God has sent you to set up the kingdom," she murmurs.

And now Elijah Pierson, and his friend Mills, and Isabella are immersed in the business with Matthias of setting up the "kingdom." The way has been opened for the prophet as if he had dropped out of a page of Ali Baba. His patrons and Isabella had been waiting for just such an event as the arrival of the extraordinary Matthias. His

name suggested Matthew, and sounded remarkably close
to Messiah. His body, form, verbal expression, and manner—all fitted him exactly for the rôle which these people
had been praying for someone to fill; and he had the
temerity or the imbecility to essay the rôle.

Not an idiosyncrasy of Pierson or Mills but what this
man goes a step further; not an idea or expression of theirs
but what he advances a more phantasmagorical idea. Pierson had received a call to become Elijah back in June,
1830? Quite so. On the identical day, Robert Matthews
had become Matthias—Matthew, the Messiah and God all
in one.

The two old gentlemen and Isabella, in their eagerness
to create the Creator, divest themselves of their worldly
possessions and, throwing them at this impostor's feet, in-
vest him not only with plenary power over their wealth as
well as their very bodies, but with every attribute of the
God-head. He is a being of surpassing excellence, of inexhaustible wisdom and light, possessing all power and
knowledge, whose business it is to establish the personal
reign of God the Father on earth.

Behold now the raiment of the prophet as he dines at
the table with his disciples. With money from Pierson and
Mills he has purchased for himself a gorgeous robe, on
which hang suspended twelve large silk tassels, representing the twelve tribes of Israel. Around his waist is an
elegant red silk sash. As he sits with his guests at the table,
imposing in these garments, his long beard does give him
the air of a prophet, albeit a prophet of doom. Everything
is solemn and orderly. Everything has a ritualistic significance. But everything redounds to the glory of Matthias,
even the silver goblet out of which he sips water, while
the disciples round about him content themselves with
drinking out of plain glasses.

No need now to go about town clad in unkempt raiment,
or seated on a nag. There is a change of raiment for every

day of the week; and when he rides it is in a superb dark
landau drawn by a noble pair of horses, gorgeously capari-
soned. He is still the Matthews of old, however, for wherever he goes, be it among the brokers of Wall Street, or at
some corner bookstall, or at the Battery where he loves
to promenade, he cannot resist preaching and exhorting
and hurling figurative coals of fire and brimstone at the
multitudes who follow him more to look upon him than
to listen to what he may say.

He is alighting now from his carriage, in a wide-open
spot on the Battery where he may be seen by all. He is
clad in a black cap of japanned leather, shaped like an in-
verted cone with a shade, and around his neck is a black
sock. His Wellington frock coat is made of the finest bottle
green cloth, lined with pink satin, and richly decorated
with braid and frogs and costly buttons. Underneath is a
vest of figured silk, and around the waist a crimson silk
sash. This day he is wearing green pantaloons with sandals,
but he really has a penchant for white or black pantaloons,
and usually sports highly polished Wellington boots, which
are worn outside the pantaloons.

Does anyone wonder that, a little later when a choice of
residence is involved, Isabella chooses to accompany the
flashy Matthias rather than remain with the plainer, more
sober Elijah Pierson?

And what, precisely, is this man saying which so completely captures this company of people who literally fall
upon his neck or rest in his bosom and give heed to his
words?

Here is some of the drivel:

"Our creed is truth, and no man can find truth unless he
obeys John the Baptist [meaning Pierson, who becomes
alternately Elijah and John the Baptist], and comes clean
to church."

"They who teach women are of the wicked."

"The communion is all nonsense; so is prayer. Eating a nip of bread and drinking a little wine won't do any good."

"All females who lecture their husbands—their sentence is, 'Depart ye wicked, I know you not.' "

"Everything that has the smell of woman shall be destroyed."

"In a short time the world will take fire and dissolve—it is combustible already."

"When you see anyone wring the neck of a fowl instead of cutting off its head, he has not got the Holy Ghost."

"If you eat a piece of pork it will go crooked through you, and the Holy Ghost will not stay in you, but one or the other must leave the house pretty soon. The pork will be as crooked in you as rams' horns, and as great a nuisance as the hogs in the street."

How seriously this man was taken by Mills and Pierson and Isabella is quite evident in a brief letter which Mills wrote to Pierson in July, 1832. It reads:

JOHN THE BAPTIST, OR DEAR PIERSON:

. . . The angels of destruction are making dreadful havoc, but do not be troubled; they are reaping the tares. The harvest is begun, and not a single blade of wheat can fall or be injured.

Katy is well, and at the "Lord's house" often.

Isabella is also well.

Matthias is still with us, thank God! and I think we can no longer say, "*when* he, the Spirit of truth is come," etc. Surely this *is* "the kingdom of God."

It is a good time to look to Pierson. What has become of his ascetic ways, his fasting, and praying, and watching?

All is completely transformed. Anyone who had seen Pierson a few months before, when he was on the brink of the grave from starvation, would not recognize the man

to-day. His face has a vigorous glow and, in place of the
pallor of anemia due to fasting, we see a man who glistens
with health, yet whose eyes contain that same fanatical
gleam which characterized the former days. But they
gleam even more fervidly when the Master turns to him
and commands, "John the Baptist, read the tenth chapter
of Revelation!"

Matthias has turned the fasts into feasts. Every Sabbath
he preaches to his followers, and those who choose may
remain to partake of the sumptuous repast which he has
ordered. Pierson had always preached "all things in common"—and now Matthias was putting the preachment into
practice. He encouraged Pierson in the belief that the
good things of life were for enjoyment, and that the time
for abundance was at hand. As long as the food they ate
could be classified as plain, they might eat vigorously and
sumptuously. But there must be no pies, no wine—and, an
after thought (he was a Jew)—no pork.

For some time Matthias lived in the home of Pierson,
sharing Isabella as his personal servant and helper. As a
rule inmates and visitors treated him as if he were a descend-
ant of royalty; but occasionally someone expressed dis-
agreement, and this was bound to elicit fire and brimstone
from the contemptuous prophet.

In one instance, however, Matthias came off second
best, and it came near destroying the kingdom. A man
who rented part of Pierson's house for a school found the
prophet more than he could accept. He flatly pronounced
him an impostor and, when Matthias heaped coals of fire
on his head, he advanced towards the bearded gentleman,
shook him thoroughly, pushed him none too gently upon a
sofa, and then—indignity of indignities—pulled the grand
patriarch's beard!

This was more than God's chosen one would tolerate.
He picked himself up, bag and baggage, and transferred

to the domicile of his friend Mills. The most significant thing about this incident is that Isabella moved with him. Perhaps Pierson, out of the goodness of his heart, loaned his most valuable servant to Matthias. He would have given the prophet his head just as readily. Then again, there is a very great temptation to believe that Isabella followed Matthias into his new home because she believed that he was God's anointed.

§ 3

Matthias had his heart set on a stupendous project.

He knew that Pierson and Mills were ready to support him in anything. Since they would spare no expense or pain to achieve the "kingdom" for which their hearts were yearning incessantly, why not just that?

But the way must be prepared.

"My kingdom," he now preached to them, "like Aaron's rod, will swallow up all other sects and kindreds. The earth will be renovated. The spirits of the apostles and patriarchs will be reanimated in other bodies.

"At present I and John the Baptist are obliged to fill a variety of offices, but in a short time men will arise to occupy the different posts so that there will be again twelve apostles and twelve patriarchs.

"This is the era of the First Resurrection. God has established the railroads in order to prepare the way. The sea will be covered with dry land. There will be no more cities. People will live in palaces, scattered over the land, riding in elegant carriages and dressing and living in wealth and splendor."

To which Pierson and Mills and Isabella shouted, "Amen."

Now he is ready for the great project, the project which will fulfill all those dreams which Pierson has had for many years and which he has impressed upon Isabella's mind and imagination.

"We shall build the New Jerusalem," the prophet announces. "God has commanded me to build it in the western part of this state. It will be more magnificent and more beautiful than the Greeks or Romans ever knew. Out of the ocean will come long concealed treasures to be placed in it. All the tools and implements and vessels in the New Jerusalem will be made out of massive silver and pure gold.

"In the midst of the city will stand an immense temple far grander than Solomon's. Around the central temple will be several smaller ones. I will sit enthroned in the great temple, John the Baptist will occupy one of the lesser thrones, on the right, and Mills will occupy the one on the left.

"Before me is to be an altar with a massive candlestick, containing seven branches, and made all of pure gold. Before John the Baptist and Mills shall be altars also, these equipped with iron candlesticks. And there must be furniture to correspond."

The kingdom is all astir. Surely God has come to earth again. Elijah Pierson is his prophet. Mills is a lesser prophet, and Isabella is their handmaid. Glory be to the Heavenly Father!

"The kingdom must be equipped with silverware and other plate," thunders the now insatiable Matthias.

With Mills he enters the store of a silversmith on Broadway for the purpose of examining silverware for the New Jerusalem.

"It is now the reign of the Lion," the prophet roars to the proprietor of the shop.

"The British lion?" queries the innocent silversmith.

"No," explodes the priest of God, "I mean the lion of God."

To the astonishment of the shopkeeper, who is acquainted with Mills, he is informed that the Mills familyplate is to be altered to contain the inscription, "The Kingdom of God is at Hand."

He knows that Mills is not jesting, for on the succeeding day he returns bringing a huge basket of silverware, including an entire tea set.

"I want a silver lion placed at the top of every piece," Mills instructs the shopkeeper, who stands aghast before his customer, "and out of the spout of the tea-pot I want a lion's head to emerge, out of which tea may be poured. ... And on this silver chalice, inscribe, 'Presented to Prophet Matthias by ——— Mills and his children.' "

Now the silversmith is positively alarmed, and secretly conveys word to a brother of Mills and to other relatives that he has gone insane and that on account of Matthias he is about to squander his entire fortune. These relatives take the hint immediately, and proceed directly against the Mills establishment. Together with members of the police they enter the merchant's home. There they find Matthias, Mills, and Isabella.

Mills was led away gently, and there was no disturbance. But when they advanced to secure Matthias, they reckoned without Isabella. She stationed herself between her Master and his pursuers and fought off each attempt to reach him. Andrew Mills, the merchant's brother, violently struck her finally, and then forcibly put her out of the house. In a moment, however, she had returned, much to the consternation of all present. She was evicted again, and still she returned. This incident recurred several times before Matthias, who all the time had accepted his plight with philosophic calm and humility, could be bundled off.

"They are crucifying him," exclaimed Isabella, no doubt imagining that the same fate which overtook the Messiah was now about to come to Matthias.

Thanks to Isabella and Pierson, Matthias was soon free. But this ended the stay of the kingdom in New York City proper. Soon all activities were transferred to "Zion Hill," located at Sing Sing, New York. Mills had seen the error of his ways and had left the fold, but Pierson and Isabella soon followed their Master to his new retreat. Others went along also, including a certain Mrs. Folger and her husband, Benjamin Folger, who was a rather prominent New York business man.

The arrangement at Zion Hill was strictly communal. Pierson had induced Isabella to place all her savings in a "common" fund, and whatever furnishings she had acquired, she added to the equipment of the kingdom. She received no wages, and was not looked upon as a servant, although her tasks were menial in character. Matthias was represented as the "Father," Pierson was still John the Baptist or Elijah, and later on Mrs. Folger became "Mother." (What an amazing resemblance to a recent New York cult!) Isabella's work was in the kitchen. Mrs. Folger assisted in the light housework. Pierson busied himself with farming, and a daughter performed light housework. Matthias did whatever it pleased him to do, which usually consisted of preaching, praying, or fulminating against some imagined evil.

For a while the place was bathed in holiness. The work in the house or on the farm consumed much of the time. There was no regular time for worship, and such worship as they engaged in was quite informal, consisting chiefly of prayers which might be shrieked to the heavens at any time and under any conditions; and of course Matthias preached at every opportunity.

But peace was not to reign for long. Matthias, who had convinced his followers of almost every kind of absurd view or practice, acted upon Pierson's obsession to return once more to his deceased wife by announcing a doctrine of "matched souls." No one was married truly, he stated, unless he was matched spiritually with his mate. On this basis Pierson was due to meet his wife again in the form of some person who possessed his soul-match, and on this basis, too, he, Matthias, had the right to dissolve the ordinary type of marriage.

But Matthias had a deeper motive than he at first revealed.

One day he announced to the group that he and Mrs. Folger had discovered that she was not matched, spiritually, with Benjamin Folger, but that he and Mrs. Folger were soul mates and must become man and wife. Before members of the kingdom could regain their senses, even Folger, who was passionately devoted to his wife, nevertheless was convinced, and plans were made for the new marriage. Pierson performed the ceremony, and Benjamin Folger gave away the bride!

From this point on, the story of the kingdom becomes too sordid to detail here. The House of Zion developed into a place of riotous carnality, involving all members except Pierson and Isabella. Pierson had become an invalid, and Isabella has admitted that her escape was due chiefly to the fact that it was not possible to find a "match-spirit" for her in the kingdom; for, believing in Matthias as she did, she was no more proof against his perverse teachings than the other members of the group.

Pierson's invalidism probably resulted from his neglect while Matthias was making love to Mrs. Folger. He developed epileptic symptoms and, as time went on, the attacks became more frequent. While his health was declining, Matthias steadfastly refused to permit a physician to enter the kingdom, insisting that God never intended for members of Zion to require medical attention. Pierson got steadily worse until, after a loathsome period of mental and physical helplessness, he expired.

Now a terrible thing befalls Isabella. Soon after Pierson's burial relatives, suspecting foul play, cause the body to be exhumed. Evidences of arsenic poisoning are disclosed and, on suspicion of murder, Matthias is arrested. But Isabella has been the most devoted servant and admirer of Matthias. Was she not his accomplice in the crime? Thus the rumor has it.

Not long after, Benjamin Folger and his wife, who by this time have become reconciled and have turned against Matthias, add a second rumor; namely, that Isabella has attempted to poison the entire Folger family!

Alas, Isabella, you have come to a pretty pass through your devotion. Crimes like these have been heard of among the witches and conjure men of Asia and Africa, who go to great lengths with their fanaticism. What have you to say to all this?

We have brought to light all the relevant facts because, in any life of this woman, all interested persons will want to know the truth about this period in her experience. Was Isabella an accomplice in murder? Was she guilty of attempting to murder by poison?

Some already have answered yes to these questions, but the weight of evidence to the contrary is so enormous that anything but a negative answer is preposterous.

First of all, Isabella never was arrested on either suspicion, although Matthias was arrested and tried on the charge of murdering Elijah Pierson. It needs no great imagination to infer that the evidence against the Negro woman must have been so flimsy that it could not even be propped up; for whoever heard of a Negro, accused of murdering a white person, failing to get arrested?

We have collateral evidence vouching for the character of Isabella in the form of eight letters from former employees, including John Dumont and Isaac Van Wagener who, when they learned from her that she was under suspicion of having committed grave crimes, willingly wrote in her behalf.

"Faithful, honest, industrious . . . always known . . . to be in good report by all who employed her . . . ," says Van Wagener.

"Always . . . perfectly honest . . . ," writes Dumont (this is very important), "and we have *never* heard anything disparaging against her since she left here, until I heard this" (remember, this is Dumont, from whom she ran away), ". . . on the contrary, I have always heard her well spoken of by everyone that has employed her."

"She merited the entire confidence of my family, by her good conduct and fidelity," writes A. Bruyn Hasbrouck, of Kingston.

And others said:

"We do state that we never had a servant that we could place such implicit confidence in."

"A strictly honest, moral woman, and her equal I have not found since she left me."

"Faithful, honest, and looked to everything with more care and prudence than could be expected from a woman in her capacity . . . . has ever borne a character superior to her color."

"We never have had a servant that did all her work so faithfully, and one in whom we could place such implicit confidence—in fact, we did and do still, believe her to be a woman of extraordinary moral purity."

The significant note in all these letters of recommendation is that of honesty and probity. One may have a moral lapse, but consistent liars are born, not made overnight. Consequently, much credence must be attached to Isabella's own testimony in which she contends that the "poison" stories were fabrications made out of whole cloth, and manufactured by persons who had private reasons for shunting an unsavory episode into her lap.

But there is still greater weight of opinion in her favor.

If you will investigate the literature published in America during the year 1835, you will find two volumes bearing the title *Narrative of Isabella*. These were written by a New Yorker named Vale who, sympathizing with Isabella's plight, decided to expose Matthias as an impostor, and at the same time vindicate Isabella.

This is the man who noted that Isabella was about thirty-eight years of age at the time. He questioned Isabella thoroughly and repeatedly, and discovered that not once in a dozen or more repetitions of any incident having to do with the kingdom did she deviate from her original story—a pretty fair test of the validity of her defense.

Now why would a white man in 1835 attempt to vindicate a none-too-prepossessing female Negro, only recently released from slavery, unless it be that he had been so stirred by an injustice (as he confesses) that he rises to her defense?—granted of course that there is no private personal motive, as there does not appear to be in this case.

The final word in Isabella's behalf is this: she showed no fear during the inquisition which took place, made no attempt to run away from the scene, and conducted her part of defending herself in the most dignified, intelligent manner conceivable.

First of all, she procured one of the ablest attorneys in New York City to defend Matthias, to whom she remained loyal to the last; and, when this man had obtained his freedom, she, a black woman and former slave, entered suit for slander against Benjamin Folger.

Recall that Isabella had not once been arrested, nor was she likely to be. What had she to gain by instituting suit against Folger? Vindication perhaps; but was there not greater risk of losing the suit, and even of becoming involved again in the Pierson affair, the details of which Folger knew about as much as anyone?

Surely no Negro woman in her right senses, if she were guilty of the crime of poisoning a well-to-do white family, would be foolish enough to enter suit for slander before she had been formally accused of the crime. Either Isabella had infinite gall, or she was insane, or she possessed the anger of innocence.

We admit that she did not lack courage (as this act indicates), but this does not imply gall. She gives no evidence at this time of being insane, albeit she was a religious fanatic. We are forced to the opinion that it was righteous indignation that prompted her to initiate suit for slander against Folger; and we are mightily buttressed in our belief by the fact that a white jury not only vindicated her plaint, but adjudged her worthy of one hundred twenty-five dollars' damages against the well-known business man, Benjamin Folger—no mean sum in those days.

Thus ended the Matthias Delusion, as the incident became known during and after the sensational trials.

When the furor had abated, all the members of the kingdom had scattered to the four winds, including Pierson who had gone into his long sleep, and Isabella who returned, weary and considerably shaken, if not actually disillusioned, to New York City, where she received immediate employment in the home of the respectable Whiting family.

§ 4

Life must have appeared strange and prosaic after the experiences at Zion Hill.

Two difficulties immediately confronted her. She had no funds, because everything that she once possessed had gone, at the suggestion of Elijah Pierson, into the kingdom, and this of course had disappeared or been confiscated.

But the harder problem was that of rehabilitating her

reputation. Here was a formidable difficulty. The entire kingdom episode was shot through with corruption and moral turpitude. Any way you looked at it, it had an un-savory character. We have seen Isabella vindicated of all complicity with its grosser evils, but she herself has ad-mitted that it was her lack of feminine charm rather than will power of her own which saved her from the more sordid contaminations which engulfed other members of the group.

It may as well be acknowledged here—and to Isabella's advantage—that up to the time of this experience she was a reasonable dupe for such a fantastic show. Her mother had nursed her in an atmosphere of mysticism. Her days with Scriver, impressionable days when she lived with people who were just as "earthy" in a pagan way as Matthias and his followers were in a far more sordid man-ner, probably had never been completely erased from her mind. Her life at the Dumonts' was a continual struggle between acquiescence to conventional attitudes of eco-nomics and morality, and the contravention of these atti-tudes through the force of her amazing personality and individuality.

That she should, immediately after arriving in New York City, become deeply engrossed in religious matters indicates clearly the trend of her temperament. And that Elijah Pierson should have seized upon her right away to become a partner in his kingdom is proof positive of a certain mystical affinity which she possessed for such people and such attitudes as Pierson and Matthias repre-sented.

Let us be calm in the matter. Here is a Negro woman, age thirty or thereabouts, who all her life has heard about the bearded prophets, and more latterly about the Messiah. Endowed with an especially keen mind which makes her ask questions and determine to get along in the world, she seeks at the first opportunity to get free of her slave

shackles. She succeeds in this, and soon thereafter decides
to go to the great metropolis. Strong in body and spirit,
she has hardly arrived in New York City before she is
outpraying and possibly outpreaching her compeers, and
even "betters." Thus she attracts attention, and the merchant Latourette seeks her assistance in his private religious
work. In this way she makes the acquaintance of Elijah
Pierson who, by his easy, gentle, confident manner, im-
presses her with being an outstanding exponent of heavenly
wisdom.

Remember, this woman has met few persons who have
taken an interest in her in these matters, and usually they
have been ignorant or coarse, or both. In Elijah Pierson,
however, she met a person possessing all the sweetness of
the mystical Jesus; and besides he rang with prophecy.

When the matters about which Pierson constantly uttered assurances, and the spiritual edifice which he had
visioned, suddenly seemed to flower in the phantasms of
the bearded Matthias, small wonder that this unlettered
woman swallowed that gentleman—to use the vernacular
—hook, line, and sinker.

He gains an ascendancy over her which eclipses all
reason; but then did he not dwarf both Pierson and Mills,
and this by their own consent?

Isabella soon becomes one of his most devoted followers.
Nothing that he does or says is wrong, even though in the
latter phase of the kingdom she does begin to develop
doubts and misgivings. Even her doubting is of the waver-
ing variety, however. And naturally so. For her seriously
to doubt Matthias was to forfeit everything which she had
created in her mind about the divinity of Matthias and of
his kingdom. It is just as much to ask Isabella to forsake
Matthias as it is to demand the average religious believer
to renounce his God: all of life has been built around this
belief, and to live without such belief is as near a living
death as anything can be.

Therefore Isabella clung to Matthias, even though she could scarcely believe that God's kingdom condoned some of the things which went on at Zion Hill. She went even further for, at every point where it became necessary to rescue Matthias, lest outside enemies trap him while he was engaged in some questionable activity (as when he had his affair with Mrs. Folger), Isabella sounded the alarm. This was entirely in keeping with her belief in Matthias and her faith that his kingdom was the true kingdom.

There are some who will contend that Isabella's worship was plain idolatry or, worse, mere infatuation. The point is relatively unimportant. Religious fanaticism is often characterized by just this kind of infatuation. It may be that the essence of religion, related as it is to the life-conserving elements of the universe, is associated with the forces which create life, with the result that religious zeal and warm personal devotion are naturally to be found together. The important point is this: Matthias and his kingdom held Isabella for the very reason that all her life she was a devoted believer in religious mysteries.

The more you look into this affair, the more astounding is the outcome where Isabella is involved. Are not the eight character references astonishing tributes, all things considered? Is it mere accident that she secures employment with a reputable family immediately after the Matthias trial and her own suit against Folger?

But the most remarkable result is the two volumes written largely to vindicate her. Here is one of the most singular instances of regard for a Negro in all the history of the race in America. What makes it still more remarkable is the fact that even while Vale penned his words, slavery was the lot of the vast majority of Negroes in the United States. That this white man should have chosen, first of all, to accept Isabella's testimony on a plane of equality with that of white witnesses, only to go still further and dare to defend the black witness on the ground of the more certain veracity of her testimony when compared with that of the white witnesses, is almost unbelievable. If any proof in addition to the jury's verdict against Folger is wanted of the unusual qualities of this woman, it is these letters of recommendation after she had become a storm center in the Matthias controversy, and the two volumes by Vale.

The astute courage of the woman never was more brilliantly demonstrated than by the method she employed in procuring complete vindication. Shortly after the charges by Folger that she and Matthias had poisoned his family, with the result that Elijah Pierson's body was once more exhumed, Isabella went to Morristown, New Jersey, where some of Pierson's friends lived, in order to justify herself with them. There, however, she encountered open suspicion and hostility. Repeatedly, former friends implied that she had been involved in an attempt to poison Benjamin Folger's family.

No attempt was made, however, to arrest her. Why, then, did she not take the easy way out and leave the terrain behind her? The simple fact is that she was too intelligent and too courageous for anything like that. In the first place, Matthias was in prison; she must help him. Secondly, she knew that she was right. Her God had extricated her from similar narrow places; why not from this one? The results confirmed her faith: Matthias was released, and she obtained one hundred twenty-five dollars' damages from Folger.

Her God had not forsaken her, even if she had made a few mistakes. The enemies of this former slave might persist in their malicious beliefs about her activities at Zion Hill, but certainly Jehovah would make them realize it was dangerous to publicize their suspicions!

§ 5

Little is known about Isabella's affairs during the next few years. Doubtless the Matthias episode haunted her for a long while. It can hardly be imagined that the effects of those years were quick to wear away.

She lived now with her son Peter, who was in his 'teens, and her little daughter, seven years of age. She might have remained in New York City with her children indefinitely, but two factors intervened to change the course of her life. The first was her son.

What had become of this boy during the time of her sojourn at Zion Hill, we have no way of knowing. Probably he and his little sister stayed in the care of friends or relatives, possibly some of Isabella's older daughters, or perhaps with her sister Sophia. It seems quite certain that they were not with her at Sing Sing. We do know that after the kingdom was dissolved she took care of them herself.

It was probably at this time that she discovered that all her devotion to affairs in God's kingdom did not mean, necessarily, that the future of her children was assured; for though she now took these children with her to religious meetings, and talked with them and prayed over them, or scolded and even whipped them, still the boy, at least, could not be restrained.

Quite naturally. He was of another generation, and for the most part a free generation. Isabella might have known better than to trust only to prayer meetings for the welfare of a son in New York City. Peter was developing into a tall, attractive, and active lad, endowed with a quick mind and a cheerful disposition. He possessed all the requisites of a nature that could succumb easily to gay life in a big city, for he was in addition frank, generous, and fond of the lighter things of life.

Yet his mother knew nothing with which to counteract harmful influences except prayer meetings and scoldings.

Worse still, Isabella, with her energetic mind and body, must constantly have been away from home, attending a thousand and one meetings of every description, "saving" the world from destruction; and all the while the son under her own roof was going to demnition bowwows. It is one of the ironical facts in an individual's devotion to a cause, particularly in the case of women, that frequently the blessings which are promised for sincerity and loyalty escape the children. The reason, of course, is obvious: the parent cannot take time to attend to the children.

Peter was far too clever a boy to be left at home alone without a father, or at least an older brother, to guide him. For two years he had been free to go about New York City, of all places, seeking out the dives and other haunts of questionable amusement. For purposes of deception, he even went so far as to adopt the name of a Negro barber, Peter Williams, in the event that he should be called to account by the law for some of his activities. Isabella, rapt in her praying and preaching, knew nothing about all this; she imagined that her boy was plodding along earnestly, ultimately to carve a niche in fame by means of his clever mind.

A friend of Isabella's, a lady of considerable means who was fond of Peter because of his generally nice manners, offered to provide him with an education—an unusual opportunity for a Negro boy even in free New York. Since he was fond of ships, she paid his tuition in a school of navigation. For a while Peter pretended that he was attending this school; the truth is that he was using absence from home to go to school as a pretext for attending dancing classes. The ruse was eventually discovered.

Perhaps he would become more steady if he had employment. The good friend obtained an excellent position for him as a coachman. The consequence of this move came near being prison for Peter for, at the first need of money, he sold his livery and other property of his employer. Fortunately, he was not arrested, but his employer, attracted also by the boy's engaging manner, merely released him from his position.

By this time Isabella's eyes were opened to the serious- ness of the situation. Assuredly life in a great city was not all that it promised to be. This boy was getting her into one embarrassment after another. The saddest part of it all was that he was caught in a vicious circle: his easygoing temperament led him into mischief, and it likewise made easy his release from punishment. The result was that Peter grew more and more disrespectful of the law. He would listen quietly while his mother admonished him, never sulking, always the first to confess his error, and ever ready with a promise of reform. But in no time he was caught up again, and was squirming out of the new difficulty by the usual tactics.

What to do? What to do?

This was an awkward complication for Isabella after all the previous troubles. If these conditions persisted, her boy was certain to be involved in some awful crime, thereby adding further notoriety to the family name. From day to day she lived in mortal dread of learning that the impending doom had come down upon her house.

He was interested in ships; perhaps he could be induced to go to sea. The rough life on the ocean would make a man of him. Certainly he would be in far less danger than from the dives of the city. If only he would go aboard a government warship! That would teach him discipline, and the respite would give him time to take hold of him- self.

She confided her wishes to him. He listened to her with the same courtesy, made his customary promises, broke them as usual, and soon was consorting once more with his old cronies.

Isabella was desperate. There seemed to be no way out

for her. Was this a curse from heaven? Some retribution for the idolatry at Zion Hill?

"But God," she prayed, "deliver me from the horror of this terrible thing. Spare me the terror which hovers over me and my child."

The story was repeated. A messenger came to her home and informed her that Peter was in the toils of the law again. Thank God it was nothing serious! But where was this thing going to end?

Isabella realized at last that the situation demanded desperate remedies.

"I will not do a thing for him," she decided, with resolution. "I will let the law take its course. It is the only way I can bring my boy to his senses."

Peter, left to his own resources for the first time since he had been with Isabella, became panic-stricken. He thought of his pseudo-namesake, the Negro barber. He remembered that he was known to come to the rescue of colored lads who were caught in the clutches of the law. He sent for him.

When Peter Williams the barber received the call from Peter Williams the prisoner, his curiosity was immediately aroused. He visited Peter at the Tombs prison, and listened to his tale of woe. When he heard that the lad had a mother who refused to come to his assistance, he was incredulous, but nevertheless he proceeded to secure his release.

Then he visited Isabella.

"I am very glad that I have been able to assist your son," he said to her after they had talked awhile. "He was in great need of sympathy and help, but I could not believe that he had a mother in the city, although he assured me that he had."

Isabella explained to him the reason for her refusal to intercede. Williams agreed to help her by arranging for Peter to go to sea. This made Isabella very happy, but she still feared that Peter would find some pretext for evading this plan before the boat on which he was to depart sailed away.

Peter this time, however, seemed very much in earnest. He urged his mother to trust him, promising faithfully to improve his ways. Isabella had serious doubts, however. Even when Peter Williams sent her a message in the early summer of 1839, saying that Peter had sailed away, she doubted it. For a month or more she was afraid that she would encounter him emerging from some alleyway or dive.

Then in October of the following year she received a letter from her son. He was at some faraway port. Another letter followed in March of the next year, and still another in September of the same year. After that Isabella never heard from or of him again. She believed that he had corrected his bad habits, and had gone to live peacefully in some distant land.

It seems hardly likely that this boy would altogether forsake his mother. The fact that she lived in one of the world's most interesting cities, and a seaport at that, makes it hard to believe that he would forever remain away from the scenes of his boyhood. It is altogether more than probable that the ship on which he was sailing foundered somewhere in mid-ocean, and carried him down.

§ 6

Life was still one difficult problem after another.

Her mind was eased somewhat by the departure of Peter, and doubtless the years had helped her to live down the ill fame of Zion Hill. Still her restless spirit could find no peace. After the exciting experiences at Zion Hill, with all the lurid promises involved in the adventure, any normal routine existence must have been monotonous and trying.

The chief difficulty was her poverty. She was no longer precisely what one might call a young woman. The exacting tasks of slavery were not calculated to preserve youth, and she was in her mounting forties. Should not she be getting a little home for herself, so that the advancing years would not catch her unprepared? Bad as slavery was, the slave did have a roof of some kind over his head, and a crust to eat. Not so the freed man. Who could tell when that machine of a body might break down and be unable to provide for itself?

She worked night and day, with the ardor characteristic of one of her temperament, trying to eke out a living and to save a few pennies besides. The story was an eternally dismal one: infinite pains for infinitesimal returns.

What a sorry outcome to a life which once had promised to make her one of the angelic elect! What a sordid travesty —and such a drab conclusion to the grand drama of Zion Hill!

Could this be that Isabella who had dwelt with Elijah and Matthew? Was this all there was to the great dream of calling out to the world, and bringing in the sinners, leading them like lambs to the fold? What a mockery! What a tragedy! She who had talked with God, and had ordered Him about, then had lived with Him and his disciples in the forms of Matthias and Pierson, to be reduced to this! And besides, her wayward son, missing now for many months, and she herself almost destitute!

She pondered over her situation. That was an unlucky day when she turned over her earnings to Pierson. You can always add something to something—"but to him that hath not. . . ."

Or had it been an unlucky day?
Was it not all merely a part of God's plan?
After all, New York *was* a pretty miserable place.

Undoubtedly Peter would not have become the source
of trouble he did become, had he not been brought up
in this iniquitous city. Why, it was nothing but a sink of
iniquity. No wonder Matthias and Pierson had come to
such unfortunate ends. Who could remain good and pure
and holy in such a place?

A den of money-changers. She was as guilty as the rest
of them on that score. For example, in the winter, if her
employer gave her money with which to employ someone
to shovel snow from the pavement, did not she arrive
early in the morning, shovel the snow away herself, and
pocket the money?

For what?

For the rainy day, of course. But after it all, what had
she to show for the rainy day? And what about that other
poor creature who also had his rainy day to think about?
Ah, everyone for himself, and the devil take the hindmost
—that was New York.

The city becomes for her a nauseous experience. Its
walls of brick and stone are contraptions to smother the
human flock, hiding the sun and shutting out the pure air.
It is a place where alleys exist for all kinds of hidden mischief, and dives abound to entice the young and the simple-
minded.

She sees the city as an abomination, a place of crass business, where money-changers hold forth, and by virtue of
the power invested in wealth, influence the destinies of
countless thousands, even millions, of men. The city by its
very construction engenders fear, for the buildings shut
out the heavens, where hope and aspiration dwell; and the
competitive struggle for existence makes everyone afraid
lest calamity fall upon him, and he find himself destitute
beside his more fortunate brother. The city, she concludes,
is antisocial.

"Truly," she muses, "here the rich rob the poor, and
the poor rob one another."

But on more sober reflection, questions arise in her mind to tempt her, "Am I not poor? Do I not need whatever I can make for myself?"

Visions flit across her confused brain. She reviews her early slave struggle. She mentally recites the Lord's Prayer as Mau-Mau-Bett had taught it to her in the old Dutch patois. She glimpses the shadow of Matthias instructing her that the time of the Lord is at hand, and that he is here to fulfill the Lord's mission.

That Matthias influence has not altogether fled from her.

"Go out into the world. Gather in the flock. Preach repentance and baptism. Tell them that a judgment day is coming and that it is near at hand."

Sakes alive! These worldly things—are they to be a concern of hers forever? Money? Food? Clothing? Houses? Drudgery?

Never.

Never. Never.

There is to be no going back to that. She could see now that all this business of preserving self, this matter of the individual's looking out for the rainy day, was un-Christian and antisocial. The question was not merely one of thinking of one's self before considering others, but it involved also the misery which might have befallen some other person who was in even greater need. The city was surfeited with the very lack of the spirit of brotherhood and social concern, instead of the love which so many people protested with their lips.

And now, money and property, instead of being essential or desirable, became for Isabella objects of indifference and even contempt. These were the things that stood in the way of brotherly love. These were the frustration of the Golden Rule.

Everything was wrong; all things in the city were corrupt and abominable. She felt like a bird in a cage, admiring

the tinsel and trappings of a little cooped-up theatre of activity, while outside the whole world mocked and jeered
at her for not coming out to play on life's stage in order
to create a society which would be a true, vital com-
munity of human hearts.

"Why do I remain here, tied down, a slave to work, ac-
complishing nothing, moving from one worry to another,
getting nowhere? What has been holding me to this one
spot, praying and preaching, working and slaving, and
making no headway? I am meant to do greater things than
these I am doing. I feel it in me. . . . . Lord, what wilt thou
have me to do? . . . . . My spirit calls me to go out. . . . . To
travel. . . . . I hear a voice telling me to travel east . . . . to
talk . . . . to tell them about the Lord Jesus . . . . to help the
world find itself. . . . . There must be persons out there
who will hear me . . . . persons who will love me and care
for me. . . . . I am not afraid. . . . . I must go. . . . . I shall
go. . . . ."

She mulled over these thoughts just long enough to prepare to carry out the divine injunction. She confided her
burning quest to no one, least of all to her children; for
she was determined not to let anyone or anything restrain
her.

One morning (June 1, 1843) she procured a pillow case,
and placed in it a few articles of clothing. When she had
finished, she went to her employer, Mrs. Whiting, and
quietly announced, "The Lord is going to give me a new
home, Mrs. Whiting, and I am going away."

"Where are you going?" asked the astonished mistress.

"Going East."

"What does that mean?" Mrs. Whiting asked her.

"The Lord has directed me to go East, and leave the city
at once," the disciple of Heaven replied.

"Bell, you are crazy!" her mistress exclaimed.

"No, I'm not," Isabella retorted.

Then Mrs. Whiting turned to her husband who was about to have breakfast, and shouted, "Why, Bell's crazy!"

"I guess not," the husband responded.

"I tell you she is," continued the excited woman. "She says she's been called away by the Lord, and that she's going to have a new name too. Doesn't that look crazy?"

"Oh, no," the husband replied. He had seen a great deal of religious hysteria in his time. He turned to Isabella and said, "Won't you sit down and have breakfast, Bell?"

But Isabella was in a great hurry.

"No," she replied, "I cannot stay. I have heard a voice from heaven. It tells me to go.....Farewell, friends—I must be about my Father's business."

III

Sojourner

DUE EAST TOOK her to the ferry.

Out of twenty-five cents or so which she had carried with her, she paid her fare across to Brooklyn. With the pillow case in her hand, she started out on foot for an unknown destination. Consulting neither books nor maps, she was guided only by the sun, now a big yellow ball in the east.

She was not in the least perturbed about the end of that journey. Was not the Lord Jesus her director, in whom she had absolute confidence for providing what she required, and for protecting her?

Her work lay before her: it was to preach the gospel and to be a sign to the sinners of the world. What more alluring prospect could her restless heart cherish than this—that it move about freely from place to place, veering like the wind, mindful neither of time nor money, giving no thought to any contingency of the future, but guided only by the need of the immediate present, to indicate how men and women could create a more social world in which to live?

She was concerned about a name, however.

Her Lord had instructed her to leave everything she had back in Egypt, and that included her old name, Isabella Van Wagener. She had cogitated a long while about this matter. Suddenly, while she was walking along a road in Brooklyn, the name came to her.

"Sojourner!"

"There, now," she said to herself, "the name has come. Sojourner. That's it. Because I am to travel up and down the land, showing the people their sins, and being a sign unto them."

She was very happy, and walked along another four or five miles. Then she felt thirsty.

She accosted a woman who happened to be a Quaker, and requested a drink of water.

"What is thy name?" queried the lady, no doubt more than a little curious about this strange Negro traveler with her pillow case, her jaunty stride, and her wide-open, frank countenance.

"My name is Sojourner," the erstwhile Isabella informed her.

The Quaker lady eyed her with some degree of skepticism.

"What is thy name?" she repeated.

"Sojourner."

The lady was still far from being satisfied.

"Where does thee get such a name as that?" she asked Sojourner.

"The Lord has given it to me," was the traveler's proud response.

"Thee gave it to thyself, didn't thee," said the canny Quakeress, "and not the Lord. Has that been thy name long?"

"No," confessed the rather startled Sojourner. Was this an inquisition?

"What *was* thy name?"

"Bell," was the laconic reply.

"Bell what?"

"Whatever my master's name was," said Sojourner.

"Well, thee says thy name is Sojourner?"

"Yes."

"Sojourner what?" the persistent woman asked.

"Oh, I hadn't thought of that," Sojourner answered, now a little flustered by this siege of questions.

The Quaker lady still was not satisfied with the name *Sojourner*. Perhaps she thought that she should have called herself Chloe, or Dinah, or something else familiar. She could not comprehend these lofty spiritual aspirations of this queer black woman. Were these not reserved for people of proper birth? Why did she have to select such a foolish name!

When the Quakeress had finished picking the name to pieces, even Sojourner exclaimed, "It don't seem to be such a name after all!"

But she was not altogether pleased by the reactions of the Quaker lady, and informed her that she had to be getting along to her friends.

"And where are thy friends?" the relentless lady asked Sojourner.

This was too much. Originally Sojourner had been taken in by the woman's kindly attitude, and her respectful Quaker manner. By this time, however, she had stirred up the old *Isabella*.

"I can't tell where my friends are," she retorted with feeling, "until I get there."

Which must have convinced the dear old Quakeress!

And now Sojourner has a new concern. She had been so happy when the voice had said "Sojourner." Why must there always be a bother?

She plodded on over the sandy road, feeling quite hot and miserable after the day's long trek and the doubts which had just been placed in her mind.

"Oh, God," the wretched traveler cried once more to the heavens, "give me a name with a *handle* to it. Oh, that I had a name with a handle to it!"

Sojourner's guiding voice called down to her, as if from God above, "Sojourner *Truth*."

The excited woman leaped in the air for joy.

"Why," she exclaimed, "thank you, God. That is a good name. Thou art my last master, and thy name is Truth; and Truth shall be my abiding name till I die!"

When night fell, Sojourner simply dropped down wherever she happened to be. If someone took her in as a guest, all to the good; otherwise she paid. She visited inns of all descriptions, and was a guest in the elegant homes of the few rich people who had Jesus enough in their hearts to discern her uniqueness, and in many of the hovels of the omnipresent poor, who possessed little else but Jesus.

Everywhere she went she busied herself with praying, and later with preaching, and in a private home or camp she did her stint of the housework. She must have been a rare sight, this Negro woman, well into middle life by now, undoubtedly appearing considerably older than she actually was; clad in a gray dress, surmounted by a sunbonnet, her figure tall and bony, her serious face lighted up by those large mist-filled eyes which twinkled mirthfully the many times she engaged in some brilliant bit of repartee; eager to pray or to preach, and just as quick to help in the kitchen or arrange a coverlet in the bedroom.

She intended, primarily, to be a teacher and a preacher. She was still illiterate, but she deferred to no one. Later in her roving career, when she wanders off to the home of Harriet Beecher Stowe just to "have a look" at her, she meets Henry Ward Beecher, whom she greets in a patronizing manner, unconsciously, of course, and to whom she exclaims, "You dear lamb! The Lord bless you. I love preachers. I'm a kind of preacher myself."

She never doubts for a single instant that the Lord has singled her out, and her of all people, to wander over the fields which are filled with the sins and the sinners of the world, and scatter His wisdom. She is the Lord's "So-

journer"—here, there, everywhere, and in everything—
and she brings "Truth." She is never daunted, because there
is no daunting the fighter who is convinced that he conveys Truth.

Everywhere she went the magic of her voice and manner produced similar results. It was not very long before
her name was being bruited about from one camp to another. With her two heaven-conferred names, she needed
no advertising manager or press agent. What could be
more natural, in a group of people composed exclusively
of white members, than the exclamation upon seeing this
extraordinary person edging forward to the center of the
stage, "It must be Sojourner Truth!"

Curiosity alone would impel groups to want to hear her.
Excitement and uniqueness are always at a premium. Well,
Sojourner's bustling manner was exciting enough, while
her appearance was unique even for a Negro. She possessed presence and emotional power which made themselves felt the instant she appeared. It was these qualities
in her that had attracted John Dumont, and then had
bound him to her. It was these qualities which had caused
men to approach her on the streets of Kingston when she
was struggling to regain her stolen son. It was these qualities which had influenced Vale to publish the remarkable
defense during the Matthias interlude.

People, therefore, were eager to hear her and to see her,
both because it was a rare enough thing to see a Negro
on a public platform, and because Sojourner was a rare
Negro.

She had a very deceptive way about her, also. Again and
again in her wanderings she put persons to shame who
were not well acquainted with her exceptional talents, and
who upon seeing her for the first time imagined that she
merely was a "freak" Negro, or an end man in a minstrel
show. These persons began by smiling, putting their

tongues in their cheeks as they smiled; but soon they were smiling differently. They left her illuminated and mystified, for now they are bound to ask: What is this new thing we have learned from Sojourner and how can such wisdom issue from that crow?

She was not always roving. It became necessary sometimes for her to stay in a place merely to rest. Invariably, however, an invitation would come to her, or an urgent request for her to visit some other place, and soon she would be off once more.

At the very beginning of her travels, when she had to wonder from day to day where she would put up for the night, a man approached her while she was trudging along a road, and asked her if she would like some work to do. She was not on any such quest, yet sojourner that she was, she went along with the man to help out in his home. A sick woman was in the house who badly needed the attentions of an experienced woman like Sojourner.

"Surely," they said to her after noting her deft manner of doing things, "you have been sent by God."

Little did they realize that this woman was there solely because she was convinced she had heard heavenly voices. But when later they attempted to induce her to remain with them, even offering her a substantial amount of money, they encountered for the first time in their lives, probably, a Negro who had things to do which were more important than waiting on table, or helping with household chores.

"I'll take enough of this money to pay tribute to Caesar," the doughty missionary told them, picking up about twenty-five cents, "but of course I cannot remain. I must continue about my Father's business."

Travel of this kind had its decided risks.
One evening at nightfall she was having notable lack of

success in her effort to obtain lodgings for the night. The stars came out, and the moon; only a dim light from the heavens aided her in her lonely journeying. After being repulsed by whites because she was a Negro, she had to flee from several Indians who might have harmed her.

Finally, exceedingly weary, she came to a large building at the end of a road, which served as a combination tavern, courthouse, and jail. There she asked for a night's lodgings, and was informed that she might remain provided she was willing to be locked in like a prisoner. Tired as she was, she demurred at this arrangement, and plodded on further.

From under an open shed sounded the voice of a woman. Sojourner went over and inquired whether the woman knew of any place where she might stay for the night.

"Not unless you want to stay with us," the woman said.

"That I would do gladly," Sojourner replied.

The woman turned to her husband and asked him if Sojourner might share their home for the night. His affirmative response was given so cheerfully that Sojourner realized that he was partially inebriated.

"I had better leave," she thought.

But she was very tired. She had refused the jail and had fled from the Indians. She could not keep on forever. The man seemed to be a pretty good type despite his liquor. She gave in to weariness, and decided to accept the invitation.

There was to be no sleep for many hours, however. The woman informed Sojourner that there was a ball in a near-by tavern, where she and her husband wanted to drop in before going to bed. She would come along, of course?

But Sojourner had no desire to go anywhere, and a ball the last place of all. It was easy to see, however, that her hosts would be offended if she did not accompany them. Nothing to do but go along.

The ballroom was the dirtiest kind of hovel where the dregs of society were in attendance. Whiskey flowed abundantly, and the fumes were powerfully intoxicating. In a short while Sojourner's hostess was completely out of her senses, and had to be stretched out on a board where she fell into sound slumber.

If only Sojourner could have slept! But there was no sleeping for her in that place. Finally, the woman's husband roused her and rebuked her for keeping Sojourner out of bed for such a long time. The woman arose and left the place, taking her husband and Sojourner with her. By the time they reached her shack, a tiny sunbeam was peeping through the farthest cloud in the east. Now Sojourner was invited to use the only bed in the room, but this proved to be a pallet so filthy that she had to decline. She sat outside the cabin, waiting for the full dawn to break; then departed in the early moments of the morning, her night having been robbed completely of sleep.

No matter. She might have fallen into something infinitely worse!

Her reputation grew rapidly.

Though she never mastered the English language so that she could speak it beyond the form of a very crude dialect, nevertheless she impressed great numbers of people of the highest degree of intellect and training. Such written greetings as the following become commonplace in her life:

SISTER—I send you this living messenger, as I believe her to be one that God loves. Ethiopia is stretching forth her hands unto God. You can see by this sister, that God does by his spirit alone teach his own children things to come. Please receive her and she will tell you some things. Let her tell her story without interrupting her, and give close attention, and you will see she has got the love of truth, that God helps her to pray where but few can. She cannot read or write, but the law is in her heart.

Back in New York City Sojourner had heard of the Seventh Day Adventists. At that time she had paid scant attention to the sect, no doubt because she was too much engrossed by the delusions of Matthias. Just now, however, at a place called Windsor Lock, the doctrines of the Seventh Day Adventists were causing great excitement. She became interested and decided to visit the camp where the meetings were being held.

When Sojourner came on the scene, the excitement of the place grew immensely. Great swarms of people flocked about the celebrated visitor in order to get her point of view.

Sojourner had learned a few things since she ran away from Dumont. If the Matthias affair had done nothing more for her, it certainly had acted as a warning to steer clear of doctrines which contained unusual interpretations of the Scriptures. Consequently, she called forth all her great canniness in order to keep from being involved in Seventh Day Adventist controversies, and still not offend her hosts.

For a while she preserved a noncommittal attitude. When they asked her what she thought about the Seventh Day Adventist principles, she replied, "It has not been revealed to me what to think." Then she made a virtue out of a deficiency. "Perhaps, if I could read I might see it differently."

But this equivocal statement failed to satisfy the worshipers.

"Oh, don't you believe that the Lord is coming?" someone asked her point-blank.

Cornered, and forced to commit herself, Sojourner came forth with one of those answers which betoken the flash of genius. In its primitive language and form it deserves to be set down as one of Sojourner Truth's most classic utterances.

She replied, "I believe the Lord is as near as He can be, and not be *it*."

Analyze this conception, and you will see that it contains the wisdom of generations.

Meanwhile, she whetted their interest and curiosity further by praying and preaching among them according to the light as she saw it. Gradually she gained their confidence.

So now this black woman, who herself had been tricked by one of the most ludicrous religious delusions on record, would employ her own bitter experiences to dispel the delusion which she was confident victimized these folk. Many of these persons represented the most intelligent families to be found in the East. Yet they stood there before this illiterate black peasant, and they hung on her words!

Wandering about over one part of the camp, Sojourner came across a large group of people who were milling together and crying out at each other in the greatest excitement. She viewed the sight with mixed feelings of pity and indignation; then, in much the same way in which she probably imagined that Jesus rushed in among the money-changers, she plunged into their midst. Leaping upon an old tree stump near by, she lifted herself above their gaze and shouted out to them, "Hear, hear!"

Instantly everyone gathered around her. She waited a moment, then began to talk, addressing them in the quiet low tones to which her voice was so well adapted.

"Children," she entreated them, speaking in a low and appealing tone of voice which sounded like a mother's croon to a child, "why do you make such a to-do? Are you not commanded to watch and pray? But you are neither watching nor praying.

"Now go to your tents. Watch and pray without so much noise and tumult. The Lord would not come to such a scene of confusion. The Lord comes still and quiet. He might come here, move all through the camp, and go away again, and you'd never know it in all this hubbub."

There was a ready response to her suggestion. A number of worshipers went away quietly; but not all. There were preachers present who violently disagreed with Sojourner. These continued to agitate among the crowd.

Then Sojourner raged within. To be sure, this was not her party, but she was present—and was she not Sojourner who brought Truth?

She defied the Adventists and rebuked them.

"Here you are," she shouted to them, "talking about being changed in the twinkling of an eye. If the Lord should come, he'd change you to nothing, for there is nothing in you.

"You seem to be expecting to go to some parlor away up somewhere, and when the wicked have been burnt, you are coming back and walk in triumph over their ashes. This is to be your New Jerusalem. [Was she thinking of old Matthias?]

"Now, I can't see anything so very nice in that, coming back to such a muss as that will be—a world covered with the ashes of the wicked! Besides, if the Lord comes and burns—as you say He will—*I* am not going away. I am going to stay here and stand the fire, like Shadrach, Meshach, and Abednego.

"And Jesus will walk with me through the fire, and keep me from harm. Nothing belonging to God can burn, any more than God himself. Such shall have no need to go away to escape the fire.

"No, I shall remain. Do you mean to tell me that God's children can't stand fire!"

And thus, Sojourner Truth, like a born warrior, you burst in, alone with your eloquence, where angels armed with the implements of heaven would have feared to enter.

§ 2

Gradually, Sojourner worked her way down East, through Connecticut, then up into Massachusetts, past Boston, and finally into Northampton, where she decided to take up a residence, and for many years after this, although she traveled about everywhere, she maintained a house there.

In Northampton she was in congenial company. There she found Samuel Hill, noted abolitionist, and George Benson, brother-in-law of William Lloyd Garrison. Many of these persons no longer found religion the only consuming passion in life, but had cultivated other great interests, notably the slave issue, woman suffrage, and temperance. Some of them, like Parker Pillsbury, were substantially atheists. But with the keen discernment and notable honesty which were her distinguishing characteristics, Sojourner Truth was quick to differentiate between the average church adherent, filled with all kinds of prejudices, and the true humanitarian, whether he believed in God or not.

And she had no difficulty making her choice. She was far ahead of her times. She was not like the present-day crop of evaders, black as well as white who, while making all kinds of concessions to the prejudices of the most bigoted people provided they profess some religious conviction, will cast completely out of the pale, say, a Communist because he is a religious freethinker. For Sojourner it meant everything that these people, believers or nonbelievers, were her friends. She loved them, and liked to be counted among them because, although they did not always agree with her great zeal for converting the world to the church, nevertheless they were the first to admire her power, her earnestness, her intelligence, and this very open-mindedness of hers.

It was these folk who contributed of their own means to

help build her a home in the vicinity; and she was made a prominent member of that immortal band which included Parker, Whittier, Garrison, Douglass, and all the other noted abolitionists. For them she became "Old Sojourner" and "Aunty Sojourner," whose fame would fly to the far corners of the country and even across into Europe.

It was in Northampton that she received a real baptism of fire.

Out in the open fields, where the pale moon was shedding a dim light over the countryside, a huge camp meeting was being held. A party of young hoodlums, intent on routing the worshipers, rushed into the camp, hooting, yelling, and making every conceivable disturbance. A hundred or more of the ruffians grouped themselves together and rushed through the grounds in every direction, terrifying the members of the meeting and threatening to set fire to the tents.

A call for the constable's forces was sent out, but in the meantime the Christians who were attending the meeting became fearful for their safety. Old Sojourner Truth was in that gathering and, despite her brave pronouncements at the outset of her mission into the world, she was among the most fearful of the fearful. In order to secure as great a degree of safety as possible she had secreted herself behind a tree trunk, where she hoped that she would be passed by unnoticed.

One can hardly blame her. She had special reasons for being afraid.

"I am the only Negro here," she thought to herself, "and as soon as these hoodlums see me they will fall upon me, and I shall probably be badly hurt."

Now the thugs were set upon destroying the props of the tent. They put their collective strength against the supporting beams, and soon the huge tent was swaying and shaking from its foundations. The terror within reached panic proportions, but no one dared to move.

Then it was that Sojourner Truth had one of those intuitive strokes which so often changed her life from its normal order. That ebullient mind of hers, which gave her no peace while she was awake, began firing thoughts at her which she could not evade.

"What!" she was thinking to herself, "am I to run and hide myself from the devil? I, a servant of the living God! Have I not heard that one shall chase a thousand, and two put ten thousand to flight? Have I not faith enough to go out and quell that mob? There are not a thousand of them here; and I know I am a servant of the living God."

"I shall go!

"I'll go to the rescue, and the Lord shall go with me and protect me."

She heard the beatings of her heart. Her heart became three hearts; her body could hardly contain them.

"Won't you go with me?" she urged several of her fellow-worshipers, as she apprised them of her intention to step outside and end the disturbance.

But none of these "God-fearing" people wanted any of that kind of horseplay.

"Then I shall have to go out alone."

She was as good as her word. Straight out from her hiding place she emerged, and to the echoes of disapproval from her friends, who called her an insane woman for attempting any such thing, she strode to the door of the tent.

See her now in the midst of the terrific noise of the hoodlums and the confusion of the worshipers. The orator who is scheduled to address the throng about the mercies of Jesus and the powers of the Almighty trembles on the speaker's stand, and the erstwhile listeners quake in their seats, terrified by the thoughts of the impending catastrophe; but this black woman remains perfectly calm. She

strides through the tent with long determined steps, her
figure aloft and commanding as befits one who believes
that Jehovah has all things in His hands. She does not hesitate, still she does not hurry. She is planning as she moves,
and she sees only one end—triumph.

Gone are all thoughts of struggles when she was a slave
on the Dumont plantation; she has forgotten completely
the brave battle for her son which was concluded with
such signal victory; so far as her mind is functioning, she
might never have been the central figure of a great religious
upheaval, winding up in murder courts and what not, in
her first years in New York City. She thinks only of saving
this meeting. But it is the Sojourner Truth whom these experiences have made, the Sojourner who has become steel
as well as tenderness, whose love for humanity has been
eclipsed only by her sure faith in an Almighty Power to
preserve her against any assault of the enemy, who reaches
out in the pale moonlight and grapples with the unreason-
ing power of a cowardly mob.

Are there a hundred of the enemy? She has a hundred
pairs of eyes to counter theirs; she listens with a hundred
pairs of ears; she feels her way with a hundred pairs of
hands. She is alert with a thousand senses, and she is ready
to seize upon any medium to achieve her purpose.

Over there, a few yards away from her, is the initial
objective. It is a small hillock of land and will make an
excellent vantage point. Before the unorganized rabble
can collect for the purpose of concentrating its efforts on
this lone Negro figure who has the temerity to face them,
she has achieved her objective, and stands now in an ad-
vantageous position above them. Many who have seen her,
draw near, not altogether certain what their reaction should
be. She has counted on this hesitancy, just as she has
counted upon their inability to form an immediate con-
centrated assault upon her position.

The din about that holy camp is unearthly. These dark

shadows flitting to and fro beneath the flickering moonlight, pushing against the tent which shakes and quivers
like a man with the palsy, give a most eerie sense of the
terrors which lurk in the darkness. A mistake with these
rascals will be fatal.

But Sojourner had known what to do the minute she
espied the mound of earth. For a moment she stood there,
surveying the motley crowd of rioters; then, with all the
strength of her unusually powerful voice, she began to
sing in her most fervid manner:

> It was early in the morning,
> It was early in the morning,
> Just at the break of day,
> When he rose, when he rose, when he rose,
> And went to heaven in a cloud.

All the young men, hearing these extraordinary sounds,
rushed towards the spot from whence they emanated. In
a few seconds Sojourner was encircled by a dense throng
of the ruffians. Peering through the dim moonlight, she
could discern scores of young fellows, armed with sticks
and clubs, who, like idlers in all generations, were out to
have a good time at the expense of anyone whom they
might intimidate. It was easy to see that they did not know
just what to make of her. They milled about her, then
seemed to pause in their tracks. At a strategic moment she,
too, paused.

Now she could make out their faces, shining weirdly under the ashen moonlight as it percolated through the dense
tobacco smoke which issued from their pipes and cigars,
gleaming in the darkness like huge fireflies.

"Why do you come about me with clubs and sticks?"
she asked in that manner of hers which was both a petition and a command. "I am not doing harm to anyone."

Someone cried back to her, "We ain't going to hurt you,
old woman. We came to hear you sing."

The cries issued from a dozen directions.

"Sing to us, old woman."

"Talk to us, old woman."

"Pray to us, old woman, and tell us your experiences."

She responded in the same quiet tones. They must have imagined their mothers addressing them.

"You stand and smoke so near me," she protested, "I cannot sing or talk."

Voices in the darkness cried out, "Stand back."

Weapons were brandished in the air. The crowd fell back, and the circle became larger. The suppliant throng pleaded for a speech, a prayer, a song, or anything she had to offer them.

Sojourner decided to speak. But just as she was about to begin, one of the boys called out, "Why don't you get up on that wagon for your pulpit?"

"If I do," she called back, "you'll overthrow it."

"No, we won't," many of them cried. "If anyone dares hurt you, we'll knock him down instantly."

Some of the lads respectfully assisted Sojourner to the wagon. Then she spoke and sang to them.

"Well," she said in part, "there are two congregations on this ground—the sheep and the goats. The other preachers have the sheep. I have the goats. . . . . And I have a few sheep among my goats, but they are very ragged."

The crowd roared with laughter. What an understanding creature!

She spoke and sang to them for nearly an hour. At length she grew weary. She took a long pause, hoping that the group would disperse, but they were not willing that she should cease.

The cries echoed and reëchoed. "More, more, sing, sing!"

She motioned to them for silence.

"Children," she said (notice the motherly attitude—with endearing phrases she disarms the enemy), "I have talked and sung to you as you asked me; and now I have a request to make to you. Will you grant it?"

A chorus responded, "Yes, yes, yes."

"Well, it is this. If I sing one more hymn for you, will you go away and leave us the rest of the night in peace?"

This took the crowd by surprise. The first response was a very feeble one. The boys did not wish to relinquish So-journer, and as for the camp—well, that was another matter entirely.

"I repeat it," said Sojourner, with characteristic insist-ence, "and I want an answer from you all, as of one accord. If I sing to you once more, you will go away and leave us this night in peace?"

The reply was a thunderous, "Yes, yes, yes."

Sojourner, the tactician and diplomat (she should have been a lawyer!), called out to them, "I repeat my request once more, and I want you *all* to answer."

Now a long loud "Yes, Yes, Yes" pealed out to the black open spaces.

"Amen," shouted Sojourner quickly, like a storekeeper with a vacillating customer, who quickly closes the bar-gain before his customer has a chance to change his mind.

In the deepest and most solemn tones of her powerful, sonorous voice, she sang another hymn:

I bless the Lord I've got my seal, to-day and to-day ....
To slay Goliath in the field, to-day and to-day ....
The good old way is a righteous way,
I mean to take the kingdom in the good old way.

Some of the young men left immediately, moving quietly out of sight under the spell of her singing. Others, however, waited. The leaders of the group then proceeded to enforce the promise they had made to Sojourner. Be-fore she had finished singing, they were all running off, like a swarm of bees, past the tents with their worshipers and preachers, and out of the camp.

§ 3

The country was seething with unrest.

It is a decade or so before the Civil War, and we wish the records were more explicit concerning Sojourner's activities. Several great issues absorb her interest. The Nineteenth Amendment is unheard of, but in her mind not undreamed. Thus it is with the Eighteenth, which will not enter into its short-lived existence for more than half a century. But the Fourteenth and Fifteenth Amendments are so near at hand that could Sojourner and her friends Phillips and Garrison realize their imminence they would faint with joy.

Even so, we catch only glimpses of Sojourner during all these most critical years. They are enough to make us sure of her mighty influence, particularly in the slave struggle, but alas! they are so scattered and fragmentary that we are compelled to supply out of our imagination and from our knowledge of the woman as she has been during her formative years much of the real drama and tremendous wealth of experience which must have gone into her years during the '50's and '60's.

Despite her illiteracy, we know that Sojourner receives numerous invitations to participate in meetings where these important topics are the prime consideration. In addition, she seems to have attended many such meetings where she had not been invited. More than once she is the unwelcome guest, interrupting the deliberations of some staid gathering by her unannounced presence, after which she listens or speaks as and when she pleases.

Her fearlessness increases with the years. Daily she becomes more relentless in her determination to fight for the "truth." Others might fear the shafts of her wit, the drollery of her epigrammatic speech, or even her very presence—she feared nothing, and least of all, physical harm or death. Her God had ordained her to speak "truth." Let

those who dared, defy that truth. Her God would settle
with them for all the rest.

Already in 1850 she is so important that a book about
her life has appeared. It proves to be a handy way to get
her story to strange groups where she can remain only for
a short while, and incidentally provides revenue for travel
and upkeep.

In 1852, while lecturing against slavery in various parts
of the East and Middle West, she decided to move on to
Akron, Ohio, where a Woman's Rights convention was in
session. Woman's Rights was an issue only a bit less un-
popular than slavery itself. Any convention of its advo-
cates was sure to attract friends and foes alike, and the
meetings very probably would develop into oratorical
free-for-alls.

Among the strongest opponents of the idea were
members of the clergy. They were in attendance in large
numbers at the Akron convention. But they and their
opposition had been expected; the meetings had been prepared with such a contingency in mind. What had not
been anticipated was a tall, gaunt black woman in a gray
dress and white collar, surmounted by an uncouth sunbonnet, who walked deliberately into the church where
the meetings were being held, and with great poise and
dignity marched up the aisle to take a seat upon the pulpit
steps.

Inevitably the rumor circled round the hall, "Sojourner!"

Surprise among the leaders speedily yielded to chagrin,
and then to open disapproval. Here was a mighty perilous
bit of presumptuousness and intrusion. . . . . Woman's
Rights nothing, their enemies would say—this was merely
a disguised abolition affair.

The buzz of disapproval was very pronounced.

Affairs became so confused that the chairman had to rap

vigorously for quiet and order. The morning session progressed like a procession across egg shells. All the while, Sojourner remained seated, quietly crouched down against the wall in a corner of the pulpit stairs, with her sunbonnet shading her eyes, her elbows on her knees, and her chin resting upon her broad hard palm. Only during the intermission did she stir, and that to interest persons in purchasing the story of her life.

But ever since her unannounced entrance into the auditorium, the convention was surcharged with the fear that at some moment Sojourner would arise to speak and thereby jeopardize the purpose for which the convention had been assembled. A constant patter of feet toward the chairman of the meeting was the result of Sojourner's presence; for the chairman must be reminded over and over that under no circumstances should she permit the Negro woman to utter a word.

"Whatever you do," they whispered to the chairman, "don't let this woman speak. It will ruin us. Every newspaper in the land will have our cause mixed with abolition and niggers. We shall be utterly denounced."

The second day of the convention arrived. Sojourner had remained so still that the fears of the group were lulled temporarily, and the two dissenting factions lashed out in open battle against each other. Various ministers called on all their powers of persuasion to pour contempt on the movement which in a later day would result in the Nineteenth Amendment.

"Why should not men have superior rights and privileges?" disdainfully asked one of these men. "Just look at their superior intellects."

Still another pointed to Jesus Christ.

"If God had desired the equality of woman," he opined, "He would have given some token of his will through the birth, life, and death of the Saviour."

"Look at what happened on account of Eve," pointed out a third preacher.

Woman's Rights was coming in for a very hard time. The timid women folk were no match for the more experienced men. They by their arguments had drawn much applause as well as sneers and raillery against Woman's Rights from rough men and boys in the galleries. A complete rout was in prospect.

All this time Sojourner Truth had scarcely lifted her head. But this was mere pose. Never had her mind been more greatly agitated, her rage more vehemently stirred. If ever she prayed to her God it was during these hours; for the trick of the ministers of calling upon the name of the Deity to condone an injustice harked back too vividly to the tactics which the same clergy was employing in a cowardly defense of slavery. For hours she had held her peace. Experience had bred a certain civility, and she would not ruthlessly trample in pastures where she had not been welcomed. But now she had heard more than she could stand. She was God's flaming messenger of Truth, and God simply would not endure a continuation of this maligning in His name!

Her mind was made up. Welcome or not welcome, she would act and act with power. Slowly she emerged from her half-hidden perch. The furtive eyes of the audience, which like the eyes of huntsmen had kept constant watch over the slumbrous dark form, were quick to perceive the motion. A half dozen voices at once gasped into the chairman's ear, *"Don't let her speak!"*

Surely the wrath of God had descended upon the meeting. At least the members of the convention thought so. It was not enough to have these ministers present, blasting away at the puerile efforts of the people who sympathized with Woman's Rights. Here, now, was the worst blow of all—woman's rights and niggers!

As Sojourner made her way to the platform, a hissing sound of disapproval rushed through the room—the kind of sound which in America only a Negro is likely to experience and understand; a sound which says, "YOU DON'T BELONG. YOU HAVE NOTHING TO DO WITH THIS."

Unmindful and unafraid, the old black woman moved on, with slowness and solemnity, to the front. Then she laid her old bonnet at her feet and, fastening her great, speaking eyes upon the chairman, she sought permission to address the group.

There she stands before the chairman, with all those hissing sounds rushing through her ears. Does she know an ounce of fear?

What!

After Nealy.....Mrs. Dumont.....Solomon Gedney's mother..... After Matthias and Folger and the Northampton thugs..... After a half century of locking horns with a hundred varieties of demoniacal opposition.... what mattered one more crowd? Who were these people anyway that they imagined they could make laws just to suit themselves—ministers, thugs, and barbarians? They with their laws about Negroes, laws about women, laws about property and about everything under the sun..... There was only one Lawgiver. He could make these picayune creatures fly, law or no law. He was on *her* side; assuredly He was *not* on their side.

She stands before the lady in the chair, looking with confident, unafraid, expectant eyes. That lady cannot refuse her petition to speak; she cannot help herself if she wants to.

The chairman turns to the audience and announces with befitting simplicity, "Sojourner Truth has a word. I beg of you to listen for a few moments."

With electrical rapidity the air cleared. The hubbub gave way to absolute silence.

Here was something unusually strange. Queer. Unheard
of. Almost inconceivable. *Impossible.*

But there she was, a black woman, unwanted, even de-
spised. Still it will be something rare to see what she will
make out of the few minutes which have been given over
to her.

Every eye fixes on the tall angular form. Her chin high,
her eyes gleaming, yet seeming more a part of some faraway body than of that quiet poised person in whose head
they shine, she stands for an instant and appraises her
audience. Then slowly, with measured accent, quietly, and
in that low deeply placed tone of voice which has made
her name a byword in hundreds of cities and hamlets, she
begins to hurl the darts of wit and intelligence which are
to leave these listeners forever changed creatures. It is one
of the few times that a speech of Sojourner's has come
down to us in its pristine form, so that we know exactly
the kind of language and dialect she employed, and what
it was in her speeches that brought people of the
highest grade of intelligence and training under her
spell.

"Well, chillun," she began with that familiarity which
came to her so readily, whether she was addressing God
or man, "whar dar is so much racket, dar must be something out o' kilter."

The audience waited with unfeigned curiosity for the
resolution which her statement implied.

"I t'ink dat 'twixt de niggers of de Souf an' de women
at de Norf' all a-talkin' 'bout rights, de white men will be
in a fix pretty soon.

"But what's all dis here talkin' about?"

She wheeled round in the direction of one of the previous
speakers. He, probably, was none too pleased to have her
attention focussed on him.

"Dat man ober dar say dat women needs to be helped
into carriages, and lifted ober ditches, and to have de best

place everywhere. . . . . Nobody eber helped *me* into carriages, or ober mud puddles, or give *me* any best place!"

She raised herself to her full height and in a voice as
rumbling as thunder roared, "And arn't *I* a woman?"

A low murmur advanced through the crowd.

"Look at me," she continued. "Look at my arm."

She bared her right arm to the shoulder and dramatically
demonstrated its great muscular power.

"I have plowed and planted and gathered into barns"—
her voice was singing into the ether—"and no man could
head me—and arn't *I* a woman?"

The murmur became more vocal.

"I have born'd five childrun and seen 'em mos' all sold
off into slavery, and when I cried out with mother's grief,
none but Jesus heard . . . . and arn't *I* a woman?"

Notice the studied emphasis of her assertion of feminin-
ity. The oratorical genius of her race is symbolized by
this unlettered woman's speech.

Sojourner perceived that the throng had been snared by
her persuasive, ungrammatical rhetoric. She felt the power
in her dramatic utterance, and she realized that she had
smashed that vague and hypocritical symbolism which unthinking white men invariably create when they choose to
boast about their deference to the opposite sex.

It was time now to launch out in another quarter.

"Den dey talks 'bout dis t'ing in de head—what dis dey
call it?"

"Intellect," whispers someone near by.

"Dat's it, honey—intellect. . . . Now, what's dat got to
do wit women's rights or niggers' rights?"

Then came one of those classic aphorisms which dis-
tinguish the creative thinker and orator from the mere
spellbinder.

"If my cup won't hold but a pint, and yourn holds a
quart, wouldn't ye be mean not to let me have my little
half-measure full?"

Now the crowd, fickle as always, is delirious. It rocks the church with applause and cheers, and echoes its approval of her words by pointing scornful fingers at the minister whom a few minutes ago it had applauded for sentiments in exactly the opposite key.

"Den dat little man in black dar," she continued, referring to another minister (she can afford now to be droll and even derisive), "he say women can't have as much rights as man, 'cause Christ warn't a woman..... Whar did your Christ come from?" she thundered at him, her arms outstretched, her eyes shooting fire. This was a lightning thrust. The throng sat perfectly quiet.

Then, raising her voice as high as it was possible for her to do, she repeated the query.

"Whar did your Christ come from?"

She hesitated a moment, poised over the audience like a bird hovering just before a final swoop down upon its prey, then thundered, "From God and a woman! Man had nothing to do with him!"

The audience was overwhelmed. It could not endure so much logic and oratory at one time. Pandemonium broke loose.

But Sojourner was not quite through. She turned finally to the man who had made a deprecating gesture at Eve, and rebuked him.

"If de fust woman God ever made was strong enough to turn the world upside down, all alone—dese togedder ought to be able to turn it back and get it rightside up again; and now dey is asking to do it, de men better let 'em."

Amidst deafening cheering and stamping, Sojourner Truth, who had arisen to catcalls and hisses, could hardly make herself heard as she shouted in conclusion, "Bleeged to ye for hearin' on me; and now ole Sojourner hain't got nothing more to say."

Thus in a few terse sentences this illiterate black woman had demolished myths which down through the ages have created vicious meanderings in the stream-consciousness of man, impeding his progress: the inferiority of woman and the superiority of certain races.

Little wonder that Harriet Beecher Stowe proclaimed her Sibyl. Posterity will hail her as one of the truly great seers of the nineteenth century.

§ 4

Most of her time now is devoted to the antislavery struggle. We hear about her wandering up and down and across the country, making speeches, giving advice, exhorting the bigoted, encouraging the weak-spirited, flaying the southern Bourbons, whipping both whites and blacks into line for the supreme conflict. To-day she most certainly would be called a "soap-box radical."

She deviates frequently. That temperament of hers, revolutionary if ever there was one, is equipped with a mind that is too keen and active, too preoccupied with a half-dozen great problems to be confined to one cause only, no matter how important the single cause. Is there a universal mind-set about some principle, a convention, or a custom? Will opposition to the convention engender open hostility or even strife? Count on Sojourner Truth to give stirring battle in the name of progress, of freedom—or as she undoubtedly would express it—of truth.

She is looking old now, much older than she really is. People are speaking of her as being in the eighties, and even the nineties. A joke spreads over the country that she was present at the nursing of George Washington. She smiles at such pieces of gossip, but refuses to be definite about her age. Somewhat later, a friend asks how old she really is and with a grin she replies, "I'm sorry. I cannot tell you that. You see, I am always looking for another chance!"

Characteristic of Sojourner. Nevertheless she is beginning herself to believe the stories about her burden of years; before her span of life has been completed she will be certain that a figure more than twenty years beyond what may reasonably be accepted is about correct.

But she *is* growing old—and aging. Only slightly, however, and there will be dozens of times when the old strength and vigor will return to transform her into a prancing steed, which comes near to being a good picture of her.

They thought she had fallen asleep near the platform in Faneuil Hall, Boston,* one night when Fred Douglass was addressing a huge throng on the slavery question. Under the spell of the great master's oratory, most people had quite forgotten Sojourner, apparently deep in slumber.

Douglass was in his most pessimistic mood. He spoke laboriously and with dejected mien about the wrongs to his people. Nothing, no, nothing could change the trend of events, he had told his audience—nothing, that is, except force. If the black man took up arms against the whites there might come a difference—but to him at that moment such a consideration was unthinkable.

The audience shared his mood. Douglass had done such a good job of convincing his listeners of the futility of events that there seemed to be little left to do except fold up tents and let nature take its own course.

Suddenly, out of nowhere it seemed, a voice boomed across the platform, rolling down into the auditorium so that no one could miss it—a voice that must have come from some place above, so clear and positive was its ethereal flight—"Frederick, is God dead?"

The effect was electrical. Instantly the whole atmosphere in that hall changed. Instead of the dejection of de-

* Fred Douglass (*Life and Times*, Boston, 1892) said many years later that this occurred in Salem, Ohio.

spair, hope filled the heart of everyone. Pessimism yielded
to unbounded optimism.

There had been no sleep in Sojourner. Tired? Perhaps.
Tired from the batterings of more than a half century of
struggle against indescribable odds. But she had not been
sleeping at all; she simply had been musing with her Lord!

In ever increasing measure grows the respect which her
fine mind and battling temperament merit despite the
crudity of her language. She is in attendance at a meeting
in a grove at Abington, Massachusetts, where she and other
members of Underground Railroad fame are gathered together to celebrate the emancipation of Negroes in the
British West Indies. Pillsbury, Phillips, Garrison, and
other notable abolitionists are present to make speeches in
commemoration of the event.

One of two former slaves, who had been rescued by the
Underground Railroad route, has just finished telling of
his experiences. A good deal of merrymaking has been oc-
casioned by the fact that his clothing is altogether unsuit-
able; for in the hurry to snatch these two slaves from
bondage, the very large one has been squeezed into a coat
which is many sizes smaller than he requires, while the
other, a much smaller man, is clad in a coat of such ample
proportions that he looks like an Eskimo or Cantonese suddenly dropped down among giants.

William Lloyd Garrison next introduces Sojourner.

"Sojourner Truth will now address you in her peculiar
manner, and Wendell Phillips will follow."

After singing a song, and saying a few things calculated
to continue the light atmosphere of the occasion, Sojourner
looks about her and says, "I will now close, for he that
cometh after me is greater than I."

To her amazement and gratification, Phillips speaks
powerfully and eloquently largely from notes he has taken
from the very carefree talk which Sojourner has made

preceding him. She is overcome by the tribute. Hardly knowing what to do or say, her mind rushes to her Lord, and addressing Him, she inquires, "Lord, did I say that? How differently it sounded coming from his lips! He dressed my poor, bare speech in such beautiful garments that I scarcely recognized it myself."

She was a curiosity wherever she went. Her color proved both an asset and a liability. People flocked to hear her, because it was such an unusual thing for them to hear a Negro speak; but they were often rude even when they did not mean to be.

One night, after she had spoken in one of the halls in Rochester, she was returning to the home of a friend. A policeman, of small stature, stopped her on the street and demanded her name. This was a surprising request and, coming from this little man, it annoyed her. She paused an instant, then struck the ground firmly with the walking stick she was carrying, and replied deliberately, in that loud, deep voice which few could imitate, "*I am that I am.*"

Did the policeman really get frightened and imagine that she was some unearthly creature? He hurriedly vanished in the night. Sojourner strode majestically homeward.

She was on one of her many forages into the Middle West. At the close of a meeting in northern Ohio, where she had made some slashing attacks against the slave-holding class, a man approached her and said, "Old woman, do you think that your talk about slavery does any good? Do you suppose that people care what you say? ..... Why," he went on, "I don't care any more for your talk than I do for the bite of a flea."

That was her opening.

"Perhaps not," she replied, "but the Lord willing, I'll keep you scratching!"

She is addressing a temperance gathering in a town in Kansas. All the while she is speaking she hears the dull thud of tobacco juice being spit upon the floor. Her habits of orderliness, developed years ago in the time when she had been a slave, have made her extremely sensitive to this form of slovenliness.

She pauses a moment and looks at the pools of tobacco juice scattered round about the place.

"When I attended the Methodist Church," she tells her audience, "we used to kneel down in the house of God during prayers. Now I ask you, how could anyone kneel down on these floors?"

She gives a vicious look at the offenders and says, "If Jesus were here he would scourge you from this place."

She has herself to defend on this score, however.

In Iowa, an antitobacco advocate, learning about her own addiction to the weed, propounds a question.

"Do you believe in the Bible?" he asks.

"Of course," she replies.

"Well," says the man, "the Bible tells us that 'no unclean thing can enter the kingdom of Heaven.' Now what can be more filthy than the breath of a smoker?"

Sojourner realizes that she is caught, but her keen mind quickly seizes upon a fitting response.

"Yes, chile," she answers, "but when I goes to Heaven I 'spects to leave my breff behind me."

Sometime later, however, she decides to give up the habit, if only to seem consistent in her own temperance stand.

Some of her roughest experiences were in Indiana. Here was a state which was undecided about the slave issue, but had strong leanings in favor of the institution. Laws were passed forbidding Negroes to enter the state, much less remain or attempt to speak there. Laws, however, unless they originated in heaven, had no terror for Sojourner.

A group of ruffians had it all arranged to frustrate her attempts to hold meetings. They spread about the town the rumor that Sojourner was an impostor, and that all her antislavery activity was a sham to assist the Republican party, which was anathema in that section. Furthermore, they stated, she was not a woman, but a man disguised in woman's clothing!

Sojourner nevertheless attempted to hold a meeting in the meetinghouse of the United Brethren, a sect in Indiana. The atmosphere was quite hostile. In the middle of her attempts to speak, a local physician arose and cried out to her, "Hold on. There is a doubt existing in the minds of many persons present respecting the sex of the speaker. My impression is that the majority of the persons present believe the speaker to be a man. I know that this person's friends do not think so, but it is really for the speaker's own benefit that I demand that if she is a woman, she submit her breast to the inspection of some of the ladies present, that the doubt may be removed by their testimony."

The wildest confusion ensued.

Many of the ladies in the house were indignant at such a proposal. It had taken most people by surprise, and enemies of the Negro woman felt as highly incensed as her friends. The suggestion was preposterous.

But Sojourner was in complete control of her emotions. She stood quietly and addressed the group once more.

"Why do you suspect me of being a man?" she asked.

"Your voice is not the voice of a woman. It is the voice of a man, and we believe you are a man." A chorus of voices had responded to her inquiry.

The meeting, thus rudely interrupted, was taken over completely by the physician and his mob.

"Let us have a vote on the proposition," he shouted—as if in a democracy even the sex of an individual could be established by means of a majority vote!

"Aye," was the boisterous response.

"The ayes have it!" and thus Sojourner was voted into the male sex.

Sojourner leaped to battle.

"My breasts," she shouted, "have suckled many a white babe, even when they should have been suckling my own. Some of those white babes are now grown men, and even though they have sucked my Negro breasts, they are in my opinion far more manly than any of you appear to be."

Then lo! she disrobed her bosom, and showed her breasts to the public gaze.

"I will show my breasts to the entire congregation," she shouted out to them. "It is not my shame but yours that I should do this. Here, then," she cried, "see for yourselves."

And as a parting thrust at the rude men, she exclaimed with fiery indignation, "Do you wish also to suck!"

She traveled to another place in Indiana, where the noted abolitionist, Parker Pillsbury, was speaking on the slavery issue. A big thunderstorm overtook the meeting. Outside, the rain beat upon the roof of the church; the wind blew with great violence, crashing the branches of trees against the church edifice.

Between two mammoth peals of thunder, a young Methodist arose and interrupted Pillsbury, who had continued speaking despite the fury of the elements. The young man was very much perturbed. Probably he knew of Pillsbury's atheistic leanings.

"I am alarmed," he said. "I feel as if God's judgment is about to fall upon me for daring to sit and hear such blasphemy. It makes my hair almost rise from terror."

And then a voice, sounding above the rain and all the

noise of the violent storm, shouted over to him, "Chile, don't be skeered; you are not going to be harmed. I don't spec' God's even hearn tell on ye!"

Fort Sumter is history.

A rather cynical friend approaches her and asks, "What business are you now following?"

Quick as a flash she retorts, "Years ago, when I lived in New York City, my occupation was scouring brass door knobs; but now I go about scouring *copperheads!*"

1862. The war is well on its way.

Sojourner has turned her footsteps to Angola, Indiana, where the proslavery spirit is very pronounced. Since she has entered the state in defiance of its laws, a warrant has been issued for her arrest. Local friends, however, have been successful in staving off the execution of the warrant.

Nevertheless, her meetings were being constantly interrupted, and she was subject to much heckling.

"Down with you," they cried out in her meetings. "The niggers have done enough. Stop your mouth."

The old *Isabella* arose in her. Fearlessly she launched out at them.

"The Union people will soon make you stop *your* mouths," was her taunting reply.

The proslaveryites attempted again to have her arrested, but the Union Home Guards, a loyal state organization, would not permit it.

Still another meeting was arranged for her at the town hall in Angola.

The proslavery group issued an ultimatum.

"If that nigger Sojourner Truth tries to speak in the town hall, we will burn the building," they said.

"Then I will speak upon its ashes," was Sojourner's unafraid, brisk retort.

The hostility increased.

Sojourner had to be escorted to the meeting by the captain of the home guards, whose prisoner in trust she became. Since the captain was in uniform, some of her friends conceived the idea of having her dress in uniform as well. They rigged her in a red, white, and blue shawl, a sash and apron to match, a cap on her head with a star in front, and a star on each shoulder.

With a fife and drum she might have masqueraded as a Daughter of the Revolution!

Sojourner looked at herself in a mirror

"The Lord help me!" shouted the sensible woman, frightened at her own belligerent appearance.

"You need a sword and pistol to complete the outfit," someone suggested.

"No, no," she replied emphatically. "The Lord will preserve me without weapons. I feel safe even in the midst of my enemies; for the *truth* is powerful and will prevail."

And now a large handsome carriage called for her. She entered, and seated with her were the captain of the home guards and several other armed men. Soldiers, too, flanked the carriage on either side, and a long, curious procession followed.

As they neared the town hall, Sojourner peeped through the window of the carriage, and saw a huge throng surrounding the building.

"These are the enemy," she said to herself. Then she prayed, "Oh, Lord, deliver me out of the hands of the Philistines."

The proslaveryites became very much alarmed when they caught sight of the armed escort, and took to their heels over the fields. But there was one who remained, a small boy, who had perched himself upon a fence and, with due consideration of youthful immunity, called out, "Nigger, nigger!"

The procession into the town hall was like an entrance into an armed camp. The double file of soldier-escort presented arms. Then the band struck up the "Star Spangled Banner," which Sojourner sang with all her strength of voice. Amidst flashing bayonets and waving banners, the party made its way to the platform.

In a few minutes Sojourner, entirely unafraid, was advocating the emancipation of the slaves with all the abandon she employed when she prayed to God. She was not interrupted and, miraculously, nothing happened. But she was advised to remain over night with the squire of the town —merely for safety's sake!

This Sojourner Truth must have been a ten days' wonder in Angola!

These ruffians had completely terrorized the town, up to the time of her arrival. Men and women alike had been afraid to express themselves on the slave issue, for fear of the certain bad consequences. Yet here was this black woman, a stranger—defiant, and making them like it!

A few persons took heart.

One friend invited Sojourner to spend some time with his family. Immediately he was arrested for entertaining a Negro! Subsequently he was released; but, while Sojourner was enjoying a respite at his home, two ladies called on her to inform her that she was about to be arrested.

"You must come right away with us," they exclaimed.

For a moment Sojourner forgot herself and rushed out with her informants. But when they implored her to hide with them in the woods, she flatly refused to go farther.

"I will not go," she said. "I'll let them take me to jail first."

The three women stood about, debating what they should do. At that moment a constable came along with a warrant for Sojourner's arrest. But in the same moment a Union soldier arrived. He informed the constable that

Sojourner already was his prisoner. This was a ruse to save Sojourner from a jail experience.

The constable, appearing very much disgusted, turned away, but not without firing a parting shot at Sojourner.

"I ain't going to bother my head with niggers," he said. "I'll resign my office first."

Whereupon Sojourner was returned to the home from which she had fled, with full military honors.

Finally, however, Sojourner was arrested. Sentiment by this time probably was against arrest, for the constable permitted her to move freely about the town. On the day of the supposed trial, the best people in Angola accompanied Sojourner to the town hall.

But by now, the proslaveryites wanted to forget all about the trial. This black woman had been a sore plague. When some of them saw Sojourner and her group arriving at the town hall, they hurriedly procured a little room and made a pretense of arranging for the defendant and her friends to wait there until the prosecution arrived.

And only a short while ago this very prosecution had threatened to burn down the town hall if Sojourner Truth attempted to make a speech in it! Now it desired nothing so badly as some graceful means of escaping from the ridiculous situation into which it had thrust itself.

Eventually, two lawyers for the prosecution, fortified to the point of intoxication for the embarrassing ordeal, presented themselves. However, one eyeful of the group assembled around doughty Sojourner Truth was more than enough for their waning temerity. They hastily withdrew to the nearest tavern for additional fortification!

That was as much of a trial as Sojourner got. She was free now to leave the town hall with her friends for a big celebration at one of their homes. The occasion was worthy of a celebration even in her eyes. Had not she, the child of

God, looked her enemies in the eye and caused them to vanish like the wind?

§ 5

The Civil War had afforded a new outlet for Sojourner Truth's inexhaustible energies.

During this period she had moved to Battle Creek, Michigan, attracted at first by a religious group which had gone out from her old home in Ulster County, New York, to a suburb of Battle Creek, called Harmonia. However, she did not stay long with these folk, but soon moved into the city proper.

Now she becomes a favorite with the soldiers stationed in the cantonments in near-by Detroit. She is the one who at Thanksgiving time proposes that the citizens of Battle Creek send dinners to the "boys." She makes frequent speeches at meetings in their behalf at Battle Creek and vicinity, and she is a constant visitor at the soldier camps, addressing the boys and bestowing gifts.

In one of the town meetings, a man whom she accosts for a contribution to the cause not only refuses but makes slurring remarks about the war and about Negroes.

"And who be *you?*" asks the astonished and disgusted Sojourner.

"I am the only son of my mother," the man replies truculently.

"Well, I am glad there are no more," is the rapid-fire rejoinder.

She is pained by the criticism heaped on Lincoln for his quiet patience and seemingly ponderous slowness during the bitter conflict. Long before the majority of her fellow-citizens realize the greatness of the President, she has detected the uniqueness of his personality and his incomparable genius.

"Wait, chile," she cautions many a severe critic who voices his fears to her. "It takes a great while to turn about the great ship of state."

Suddenly, just a few months before the war is to end, and on the brink of that critical era which will go down in history as the era of Reconstruction, this errant warrior determines to set out once more for distant climes. She will visit this Lincoln.

Yes, she had seen presidents before. She had seen them when she lived in New York. But it had always been at a distance, and this time she wanted actually to speak to one, and shake his hand. Anyway, these other presidents couldn't compare with Lincoln!

To many of her friends and relatives, this quest seemed foolish.

"You are too old, and President Lincoln is too busy. You should not go."

"I shall surely go," was her emphatic reply to the critics. "I never determined to do anything and failed."

Sure enough, in June, 1864, she left Battle Creek with Sammy Banks, her favorite grandson. By fall, after she had visited nearly everyone she could possibly see, she arrived in the capital.

It was eight o'clock in the morning when she called on the President.

Already a dozen persons had arrived to see him. Two of them besides Sojourner were Negro women.

Sojourner was just as well satisfied to wait, because she had the additional pleasure of watching the President as he actually performed his duties of office.

He was especially kind to the colored women who preceded her. One of them was ill, and complained that she was about to be evicted from her home on account of the rent. Could not Mr. Lincoln do something for her?

The President listened patiently and attentively as the

lone woman unburdened in his ears one of the thousands of petitions for help to which he was compelled to give heed.

Tenderly, and with infinite kindness he answered the distracted woman.

"I have given so much, personally," he says to her, "I cannot give more. But I will tell you where you can go and possibly receive aid."

Then he turned to one of his assistants and instructed her to assist the stricken woman.

He resumed his seat at his desk, no doubt to attend to some matters before the next interview. While he was seated, his assistant introduced Sojourner.

"Mr. Lincoln," she said to him, "this is Sojourner Truth"—the President shows signs of recognizing the name —"who has come all the way from Michigan to see you."

The President, obviously pleased by this visit, arose, extended his hand to Sojourner, then made a bow and said, "I am pleased to see you."

Sojourner responded to his greeting.

"Mr. President," she said, "when you first took your seat, I feared you would be torn to pieces, for I likened you unto Daniel, who was thrown into the lions' den."

Abraham Lincoln looked down on Sojourner Truth and said, "They have not done it yet."

Did he foresee the day, less than six months off, when the lion would seize him?

Sojourner continued.

"If the lions did not tear you to pieces, I knew that it would be God that saved you. And I said if he spared me, I would see you before the four years expired. He has done so, and now I am here to see you for myself."

The President said, "I congratulate you on being spared to come to Washington and make this visit."

"I thank God that you have been spared," said Sojourner, "for you are the best president who has ever taken the seat."

The President protested.

"Oh, now," he said, "I suppose you have reference to my having emancipated the slaves in my proclamation. But several of my predecessors, Washington, especially— they were all just as good, and would have done just as I have done if the time had come."

Sojourner would hear nothing of the kind.

"Oh," she said, "they never did anything for us. They may have been good to others, but they neglected to do anything for my race."

The President pointed across the Potomac and said, "If the people over the river had behaved themselves, I could not have done what I have done. But they did not, and this gave me the opportunity to do these things."

"Well," replied Sojourner, "I thank the Lord that you were the instrument selected by Him and the people to do it. Strange thing too, Mr. Lincoln, I never heard tell of you until they commenced talking of you for president."

"Well," said the President, smiling, "I had heard of you years and years before I ever thought of being president. . . . Perhaps you would like to see the Bible which the colored people of Baltimore presented to me," he added.

He brought out a large Bible enclosed in a walnut silver-mounted box, which had cost Negro citizens of Baltimore almost six thousand dollars to purchase. The cover of the Bible bore a large plate made of gold on which was depicted a slave, standing in a cotton field, his shackles falling from him and his hands outstretched in gratitude to President Lincoln for his deliverance. There was a scroll at the feet of the former slave, upon which had been inscribed the single word "EMANCIPATION" in large letters. On the reverse cover was another plate made of gold, on which the following words were inscribed, "To Abraham Lincoln, President of the United States, the friend of universal freedom, by the loyal colored people of Baltimore, as a token of respect and gratitude. Baltimore, July 4, 1864."

The marvelous volume completely captivated the old warrior of Jehovah. She looked through it with extreme care.

"What a beautiful book!" she exclaimed. "And to think the colored people have given this to the President of the country; and this is the country which once would not permit these Negroes to learn enough to enable them to read this book!"

Sojourner then showed President Lincoln the little book she always carried around with her, in which she was collecting the names of all the interesting persons she met. He took the little book from her and wrote in it:

For Aunty Sojourner Truth,
Oct. 29, 1864   A. Lincoln

As Sojourner bade him good-bye, he arose and took her hand, asking her to call again.

There is an apocryphal story about this visit to Abraham Lincoln which is hardly to be credited, yet which, because it has been mentioned on many occasions, we repeat here, particularly since some of the residents of Battle Creek, now living, believe that it is substantially correct.

Sojourner, according to the story, drew out a picture of herself (a characteristic performance) and said, "See, this is my picture. It's got a black face but a white back. And now I'd like one of yours with a green back, for the freedom fund."

The great President saw through the joke instantly, and drawing from his vest pocket a ten-dollar bill, he remarked, "There, Sojourner Truth, is my face with a green back."

Sojourner herself has told in detail the story of her visit to the President. She makes no mention of such an incident as this, although she does mention his regret at not being able to help the woman who was behind in the payments on her rent. The weight of evidence is against the plausibility of this fantastic tale; yet it has just enough of the Sojourner Truth flavor to allow for its possibility.

§ 6

When Sojourner Truth went to Washington, the capital was at the beginning of a period of transformation which was destined to change it from one of the ugliest to one of the most beautiful cities on the continent. Everywhere the evidences of building construction were to be seen— scaffolds, engines, pulleys, and other engineering equipment. In the process of its transformation, however, it was a very dreary sight to behold.

Most of its buildings were low, small, shabby affairs. Even the mansions of the city, usually bereft of modern improvements or conveniences, were very poor when compared to homes of similar station in New York, Philadelphia, or Boston. Every building which was not just being constructed seemed so old that it should have been demolished years before, while most of the new constructions were still in too great a state of incompleteness to satisfy the sensitive taste.

A few struggling omnibuses and helter-skelter hacks constituted most of the public conveyances. Even the members of Congress had difficulty going to and fro between the Capitol and their remote lodgings. In spring and autumn the entire west end of the city was a vast slough of impassable mud. One had to walk many blocks before it was possible to discover a single street that was crossable, which would probably be one of the most fashionable streets in the city.

There was a creek, known as Tiber Creek, which stretched out across the city. The plan was to let this stream fall in cascades from Congress House, and then have it run in three falls through gardens into the Grand

Canal. But when Sojourner was in Washington, this creek was a stagnant cesspool, oozing through green scum into the canal which, if anything, was a still more ignominious stream, a sewer in fact—a public receptacle of the city's waste, and a sure breeding place of pestilence.

Bordering on the canal, below Ohio Avenue, and between Thirteenth Street and Fifteenth Street, most of the Negro "contrabands," who had been rushed into the city by the thousands at the sound of the Emancipation Proclamation, lived in their miserable hovels and shanties. Their dwelling places were of various types. Sometimes a large one-story building would be divided into scores of these single-room shanties, each about six to eight feet square, and renting for from three to five or eight dollars per month. In these rooms two to seven or even ten persons lived, ranging in age from newborn infants to decrepit old men and women.

Usually these places were devoid of any light and ventilation. There were no toilet facilities, and the stench from the stagnant water which formed in pools outside, or in the canal, and the odors from the bodies of the inmates who could hardly keep clean if they wanted to were enough to have created a plague.

What was to be expected from such pestholes except crime, degradation, and death?

These people were bound to degenerate from bad to worse. Stripped of whatever care the master class had taken of them when they had been slaves, it was easy for them to deteriorate and engage in every kind of debauching activity. Many became lazy and shiftless out of sheer idleness. Wives and husbands lost interest in each other in the free and easy intimacy of the almost communal relationships of the dwellings. The children, left more or less to shift for themselves, roamed over the city, engaging in all sorts of petty crime, to be picked up by the police and sent to station houses, only to be released soon thereafter and ushered into lives of more serious criminal activity.

Here was a new world for Sojourner.

She was beholding for the first time the great dome of the Capitol, sublime above every other edifice in the city. Consider what that place ought to mean for all free people, she thought to herself. But what a mockery it appeared to be after one had beheld the black children along the canal!

To be sure, the war was still raging. It could still happen that the principle of liberty for all would go down before the onslaught of the Confederacy. But if Lincoln and his soldiers were victorious, would this fact alone mean a great deal for the millions of black folk of whom these thousands of unkempt, ragged, dirty, castoff people were but a tiny remnant?

Sojourner averted her gaze from the august symbol of majesty and power, and turned her attention to the miserable condition of her folk—of the black folk for whom she had struggled many good decades of her life, yet from whom she had been strangely separated.

Truth to tell, she was hardly a member of her own group. To begin with, there was a vast difference between the status of a northern Negro and that of a southern slave; but, in addition, Sojourner had been accustomed since 1830 to travel almost exclusively in white society. She was numbered among the elect with Garrison, Harriet Beecher Stowe, Phillips, Douglass, and that vast array of abolitionist stars which studded the firmament from the Quaker City to the Massachusetts Hub, stretching out over the Appalachians and across the vast prairies of the newly populated west.

She was black like these Negroes in Washington, and in one sense as illiterate as they; but all of these similarities were quite superficial. Actually she was ages ahead of them in experience, in ambition, in vision, in sophistication, and wisdom. There was as much difference between her and them, for all her deep color and ungodly English, as there was between those folk and an Australian aborigine; indeed she was far closer to the white folk with whom she associated than she was to them. It is doubtful whether she sensed the Negro in her when she was with her aristocratic friends as much as she sensed her own superior position when she was with her own folk, situated as they were in the neglected centers of Washington.

Her relative position was not unlike that of Moses who, after years of being with the Pharaohs of Egypt, trained in the highest forms of Egyptian ethics and culture, nevertheless felt the call of the blood when he saw an Egyptian mistreating a Jew. Sojourner had come to Washington a lone, somewhat aloof warrior, primarily to see Lincoln; but what she saw of her people in Washington so affected her that she felt herself compelled to identify herself more intimately with them, to remain with them, to suffer and endure with them, to help them in their extremity.

The sight would not leave her mind. It held her and gripped her. It played on her imagination in her waking moments, and plagued her dreams in slumber. There could be but one answer to all this mental and emotional turmoil: she would have to respond once more to the voice from heaven which had been speaking to her ever since she had been made aware of its existence by Mau-Mau-Bett.

Then she had been a little child. To-day she was almost seventy years old, and appeared at least fifteen years older; she herself imagined that she was well up in her eighties. Yet, despite her years—out of this vision of service, thrust upon her as it were at a time when she had come to Washington on a pleasure jaunt—there develops the crowning ambition of her very full life. Already she pictures the thing that she is about to undertake as the crowning work of her career. Age means nothing to her. Her associations with the best blood in the land mean still less. These are *her* people. She must show them the way; she must prepare the path; she must direct them.

What a woman! What a rare specimen of eternal pluck and never-failing determination!

At last, too, she has found the thing which will keep her mind occupied. For she will never rest again, until the day of her final rest, because of this urge which begins first of all as a call to duty to this segment of her people who reside in and about Washington, and ultimately develops into a "divine command" to exalt a whole people, and rescue them from oblivion.

With characteristic vigor she commences her task of "cleaning up" Washington and its environs.

What is the trouble with these folk who have rushed to the city at the first chance to relinquish their posts on the old plantations?

Well, first of all, they are filthy. Their bodies are filthy, their clothing is filthy, their homes are filthy. She had once known unspeakable conditions like these herself, when she was a little tot living in Colonel Hardenbergh's cellar; but it is doubtful if she ever recalled these conditions in her later life, so long now had she been accustomed to a life of spotless cleanliness.

"Be clean," she shouts to black folk all over the pestiferous Negro area of the city. She marches through these places in the city and in Arlington Heights, her head now clad in a spotless white kerchief, and her eyes in all probability peering through the spectacles which later life made necessary. She does not hesitate to enter the meanest hovel, nor the largest shack.

Nor has she forgotten that the best Negro forum is the church.

"Be clean! Be clean!" she cries, in one of her Sabbath

sermons to a large congregation, "for cleanliness is godliness."

She lets no grass grow beneath her feet. By December she already has received the following authority from the government:

This certifies that the National Freedmen's Relief Association has appointed Sojourner Truth to be a counselor to the freed people at Arlington Heights, Virginia, and hereby commends her to the favor and confidence of the officers of government, and of all persons who take an interest in relieving conditions of the Freedmen, or in promoting their intellectual, moral, and religious instruction.

She took steps to checkmate those whites who still made it a practice to steal back various members of the "contraband" groups and smuggle them across the Maryland border. Children were choice victims. Mothers had protested loud and long, but all they usually received for their pains was a few days in the guardhouse. Sojourner lost no time with conditions like these.

"What is the law for? What is the Freedmen's Bureau for if not to protect you against outrages of this kind? The law is for you. Take refuge behind it!"

She moved these folk to stand by their young, and to protect them; to be absolutely fearless in the presence of these vandals; and she showed them how to act and to whom to go when they desired the government to give them aid.

The Maryland culprits, balked in their game of kidnapping, threatened Sojourner.

"We will put you in jail, old woman," they threatened her, "if you do not attend to your own affairs and stop putting these people up to opposing us."

But Sojourner, who had dwelt with the finest people in America, who loved nothing more than a fight against odds, who had grown up fearing only God, thundered at them, "If you attempt to put me in the guard house, I will make the United States rock like a cradle!"

She knew what she was talking about and, what is more significant, everyone else knew. No one called to see if she was bluffing.

Under the Freedmen's Bureau, a hospital has been opened for colored folk. Just the place to initiate principles of cleanliness and orderliness! Sojourner has herself appointed to the staff which takes care of this phase of the work, and soon she is instructing nurses and physicians in the best methods of providing sanitation, order, and a clean atmosphere in a hospital.

In September, 1865, she receives the following recommendation from the War Department in charge of refugees, freedmen, etc.:

Sojourner Truth has good ideas about the industry and virtue of the colored people. I commend her energetic and faithful effort to Surgeon Gluman, in charge of Freedmen's Hospital, and shall be happy to have him give her all facilities and authority so far as she can aid him in promoting order, cleanliness, industry, and virtue among the patients.

(Signed)   JOHN EATON, JR.
            Col. and Asst. Comm.

While Sojourner was engaged in helping the distressed soldiers in the Freedmen's Hospital, she had need of the street cars of the city, which were in operation by this time. At first these operated under the rule known as "Jim Crow," which still obtains in many parts of the South.

Sojourner Truth may have been the direct cause of the change in attitude towards this practice in the street cars of Washington.

She was out with a white friend, Mrs. Laura Haviland, who proposed that they ride in the cars. Both of them understood that a Negro and a white person could not ride in the same car; therefore, when Mrs. Haviland signalled for the approaching vehicle, Sojourner stepped over to one side as if she were going to continue walking; but when the car stopped, she ran and jumped aboard.

The conductor pushed her back.

"Get out of the way," he yelled at her, "and let the lady come on."

"I am a lady, too," remonstrated Sojourner.

The conductor made no reply to this remark, and Sojourner remained on the car.

A little later it was necessary to change cars. A man was coming out of the second car as Sojourner and her friend jumped aboard. He turned to the conductor and asked, "Are niggers allowed to ride?"

The conductor grabbed Sojourner by the shoulder, and jerked her around, at the same time ordering her to get off the car.

Sojourner said, "I will not."

The conductor started to put her off.

Mrs. Haviland said, "Don't put her out of the car."

"Does she belong to you?" asked the conductor.

"No," replied Sojourner's friend, "she belongs to humanity."

"Then take her and go," the irate official said, as he pushed Sojourner up against the door.

Sojourner was furious.

"I will let you know," she said, "whether you can treat me like a dog."

Then turning to her friend, she continued, "Take the number of this car."

This surprise remark by Sojourner frightened the conductor, and he did not utter another word.

But when Sojourner returned to the hospital, it was discovered that a bone in her shoulder had been dislocated as a result of the conductor's rude treatment.

Sojourner made a complaint to the president of the car

line, and he advised her to have the conductor arrested. This she did, and the Freedmen's Bureau provided her with a lawyer to argue the case. The conductor was dismissed.

Not long after this incident, the Jim Crow rule was abolished in street cars, and there was a noticeable difference in the attitude of most of the conductors towards Negro riders.

Nevertheless, the possibility of trouble was always present. For instance, not long after the Jim Crow cars were removed, she had signalled for a car, but the motorman, observing that she was black, pretended not to see her, and went on. The same thing occurred when a second car approached. By this time the enraged Sojourner with typical ingenuity cried out as loudly as her bellowing voice would carry, "I want to ride! I want to ride!"

At the sound of this unusual yelling, all traffic in the very congested street stopped. People blocked the sidewalks to see what was happening, and carriages halted in the middle of the street. Before the trolley car could proceed on its way any farther, Sojourner had jumped aboard.

The conductor was furious.

"Go forward with the horses," he shouted at the now gloating woman, "or I will put you out."

Sojourner sat herself calmly down, then replied with all the queenliness of a visitor from heaven, "I am a passenger."

"Go forward where the horses are," the conductor thundered, "or I will throw you out."

The intrepid battler rose in all the proud dignity of a member of one of the first families of New York.

"I am no Marylander," she retorted, "nor Virginian. I am not afraid of your threats. I am from the Empire State of New York, and I know the laws as well as you."

The astonished conductor retreated at this display of self-assurance, but some soldiers who were on the car taunted him, and made a point of informing every passenger who entered the car, "You should have heard that old woman talk to the conductor."

Sojourner rode even farther than she needed to, thinking that she might as well make the most of her disputed ride. As she alighted from the car she cried, "Bless God! I *have* had a ride!"

On a trip back from an orphans' home in Georgetown, she ran as fast as she could trying to catch a car, but the motorman would not pay any attention to her, and kept ringing the bell to keep from hearing her as she called out to him. The aged Sojourner kept on running, however, and when the car stopped to admit a white passenger, she succeeded in overtaking and boarding it.

"It's a shame to make a lady run so," the exasperated Sojourner exclaimed to the conductor.

"If you say another word, I will put you off the car," the official replied and he came forward to show that he meant what he said.

Sojourner never batted an eyelash.

"If you attempt that," she retorted with her next breath, "it will cost you more than your car and horses are worth."

Whatever trouble she might have had was forestalled by an army officer who advanced and took her part.

But it was not only the officials who gave trouble.

One day Sojourner was returning from Georgetown with one of the hospital nurses. They boarded an empty car at the station, and waited for it to leave. A little while later two white women came in and sat opposite Sojourner. On observing the Negro couple, they began to whisper to each other, looking scornfully in Sojourner's direction. The nurse, who still entertained illusions about white folk, became frightened, and hung her head almost to her lap; but Sojourner gazed fearlessly in front of her.

A few minutes later, one of the white women faintly

called to the conductor and asked, "Conductor, does niggers ride in these cars?"

The conductor looked about him hesitatingly.

"Ye-e-s," he replied.

" 'Tis a shame and a disgrace," the woman said. "They ought to have a nigger car on this track."

Sojourner interrupted at this point, saucily and regally.

"Of course colored people ride in the cars," she said. "Street cars are made for poor white and colored folks. Carriages are for ladies and gentlemen."

Through the window she discerned a carriage. Pointing to it she remarked scornfully, "See those carriages. They will take you three or four miles for sixpence—and then *you* talk of a nigger car!"

The women were more embarrassed than they cared to admit. They abruptly left their seats and alighted from the car.

"Ah," Sojourner shouted at them gleefully, "now they are going to take a carriage. . . . . Good bye, *ladies!*"

§ 7

What to do?

Before Emancipation, everything had been painted either black or white. Slavery—that was the enigma to be solved, the curse to be banished. Emancipation—that was the be-all and end-all. Few people had given much thought to the gray texture of an official emancipation which, because of the circumstances in which the Negroes would find themselves, could be worse even than slavery.

Here were thousands of Sojourner's folk, destitute, uncared for, unloved, unwanted, and without any prospect of employment. Their shacks reeked with filth, and their bodies were crusty. Huddled together as they were in the larger border cities, their presence only made their situation worse, for the abstract pity of whites for Negroes whom they did not meet or see often turned to disgust and disdain when they encountered these conditions.

Something must be done.

Sojourner Truth was not alone in recognizing the gravity of the situation. However, she characteristically went ahead to solve the problem in her own way.

What about sending these folk to northern centers and letting them find work there?

This expedient would operate automatically many decades later, during and after the World War, when so great a demand for labor would arise that millions could be absorbed; but in 1866 there was no room in the North for a large influx of Negro laborers. Ah yes, the North had fought against slavery, but did a genuine dislike for slavery motivate the hearts of these folk, rather than a distaste for the form of competition which this free labor in the South presented?

At any rate, the North had little room for free black labor. Old Sojourner becomes an agent for Negro labor. She travels North and South in order to place freed men in strategic centers where they might obtain work. But what can a seventy-year-old woman do in the face of such a gigantic task?

She pauses to catch her breath—and to think.

This freedom—it is leading nowhere. Better off were these folk when they were enchained. Then they did have room and board; their clothing was provided; they were compelled to observe some forms of restraint. Even the separation of parents and children on the plantation was scarcely worse than this roaming of young folk who prowled about the large cities like homeless beasts, wasting themselves in crime and debauchery.

Ridiculous. Anything was better than slavery. At least one was free to make one's choice. No, there could be no turning back. These people with their poverty and filth were in a bad way, although all of it was preferable to slavery at its best. But something must be done.

On the one hand Sojourner saw her people, miserable and dirty. On the other hand there was the growing city of Washington, becoming more and more resplendent in its marble glory, radiating grandeur, power, wealth, and the pride of a great reunited nation.

"Who helped pay for all this?" she mused.

Negro slaves.

Oh, slavery! Fate of black folk bending o'er the cotton boll; black folk crouching in the cane brake and slushing in the rice fields; black folk nursing the tobacco weed, and rearing marble slabs to make the edifices of our nation. Black folk lending their sinews in order that the sinews of the nation may be strong and supple and teeming with life.

The Negro, after he landed on American shores, repaid more than his passage was worth. He has been paying ever since.

"America owes to my people some of the dividends."

Thus spake Sojourner.

"She can afford to pay, and she must pay. I shall make them understand that there is a debt to the Negro people which they never can repay. At least then, they must make amends."

Now unfolded before her vision the plan of a huge experiment which the nation should conduct in behalf of the Negro. Well past the seventy mark by this time, still this volcanic spirit is ready to begin all over again, with that same ardor and vigor which characterized her early days.

If only this hope might be realized!

Willingly will she work for this. Yes, gladly will she lay down this embattled head at last, and die, if only this dream might become reality.

She cannot lose time. Minutes are precious in her ebbing life! With the aid of some friends who helped her to formulate her dream in writing, she drew up the following petition which she intended eventually to present to Congress and the President:

To the Senate and House of Representatives in Congress assembled:

Whereas, From the faithful and earnest representations of Sojourner Truth (who has personally investigated the matter), we believe that the freed colored people in and about Washington, dependent upon government for support, would be greatly benefitted and might become useful citizens by being placed in a position to support themselves: We, the undersigned, therefore earnestly request your honorable body to set apart for them a portion of the public land in the West, and erect buildings thereon for the aged and infirm, and otherwise legislate so as to secure the desired results.

This was to be the crowning accomplishment of her life. As she conceived it, all the events in her career from its beginning had been leading up to this one great culminating achievement. With the help of her God she, the former slave child, reared in an atmosphere of ignorance and serfdom, would go the length and breadth of the land, petitioning high and low for enough support of her idea to induce Congress to forsake its ill-conceived scheme in behalf of the freedmen, and give them the benefit of the boon which this plan of her own offered.

"And the Lord called me Sojourner." ..... Off again she trots, now an old woman of seventy-three, though her friends are claiming far into the nineties for her; her body is stalwart and erect, her head is still high. She no longer thinks of herself as a person with royal prerogatives so much as an ambassador interceding for a people who need no apology, but whom circumstances have treated cruelly.

Now come the busiest times of her life. How an old woman, battle-scarred as she was, could move about with her alacrity and vigor must always remain a mystery. She had practically no means, and sustained herself almost entirely from the receipts which she garnered here and there from the sale of photographs of herself, or from an occasional sale of her *Book of Life*, as her biography by Olive Gilbert is called. Yet we find her traveling constantly. You read accounts of her in Providence, Fall River, Northampton, New Jersey, Philadelphia; back again in Michigan, now once more in Long Island, Boston, and even again in Ohio, Indiana, Illinois, Michigan, Wisconsin, Iowa, Missouri, and Kansas.

What a spirit!

She addresses people high and low, rich and poor. Not always now, however, are her meetings well attended.

"There was not the attendance from the male sex which she wished to see," writes the correspondent of a Fall River paper.

"A good sized audience" is the generous estimate of a New Jersey reporter.

"Rather a small audience"—we quote from a Philadelphia periodical.

The reports of her speeches vary from place to place.

In Boston she gives "a thrilling address . . . unique . . . witty . . . pathetic . . . sensible and, aged as she is . . . delivered with a voice that in volume and tone was equally remarkable and stirring."

The reaction in other places may not be so complimentary. This old lady with her "crazy" plan to tranship all the Negroes west—well, she is simply a "crazy woman," an "old mummy that ought to be enclosed in an asylum."

Hear her as she speaks in this final campaign of her long life. Note the same deficient grammar of her early years. More than ever now she has to depend upon her personality and homemade rhetoric to win over her listeners, for few will appreciate her logic. The task grows increasingly difficult with the years.

"Now, here is de question dat I am here to-night to say. I been to Washin'ton, an' I fine out dis, dat de collud pepul dat is in Washin'ton libbin' on de gobernment dat de United States ort to gi' 'em lan' an' move 'em on it. Dey are libbin' on de gov'ment, an' dere is pepul takin' care of 'em costin' you so much, an' it don't benefit him 'tall."

They were having rackets even in Sojourner's day!

"It degrades him wuss an' wuss. Therefo' I say dat these pepul, take an' put 'em in de West where you ken enrich 'em. I know de good pepul in de South can't take care of de Negroes as dey ort to, case de ribils won't let 'em. How much better will it be for to take them cullud pepul an' give 'em land? We've airnt lan' enough for a home, an' it would be a benefit for you all an' God would bless de hull ob ye for doin' it."

Note that Sojourner, for all the utopian note which may creep into some phases of her appeal, nevertheless has struck deep into the very heart of the Negro dilemma. The crux of the people's struggle, and especially the Negro people's struggle growing out of the slave issue, is owner-ship of the land. If the Negro people can be made masters over the soil which they must till, then they will be free in fact as well as in word. And Sojourner Truth under-stands this fully.

It is evident, however, that Sojourner is having a diffi-cult time making other people see this. This difficulty re-flects itself in her manner of expressing herself. Her speech lacks the more youthful cogency and wit of the speeches in the prewar era. It betrays anxiety, even misgivings, about the sincerity and earnestness of the owner-class who are in a position to make this dream come true.

"Dey say," she points out to them derisively, "let 'em take keer of der selves. Why, you've taken dat all away from 'em. Ain't got nuffin' lef'. Get dese cullud pepul out of Washin'ton, off de gov'ment, an' get de ole pepul out an' build dem houses in de West, where dey can find themselves, an' dey would soon be able to be a pepul among you.

"Dat is my commission. Now adgitate them pepul an' put 'em dere; learn 'em to read one part of de time an' learn 'em to work de udder part ob de time." (The kernel of Booker T. Washington's philosophy of education.)

May her Lord help Sojourner.

She is face to face with the stiffest proposition in her life. She bent Dumont to her will, and crushed the slanderous Folger. Singlehanded, she scotched the ruffians in Northampton, and called the bluff of her maligners in Indiana. . . . . But this *is* a proposition.

Noting the aloofness of the great white populace on whom she had counted to support her inspired idea, she waxes ironic:

"You ask me what to do for de Negroes? Do you want a poor creeter who do' know how to read to tell edecated pepul what to do? I give you de hint, and you ought to know what to do. But if you don't, I kin tell you. De government hab given land to de railroads in de West; can't it do as much for these poor creeters?" ("the railroads". . . . "these poor creeters" . . . . shades of Karl Marx!)

"Let 'em give 'em land and an outset, and hab teachers learn 'em to read. Den dey can be somebody. Dat's what I want. You owe it to dem, because you took away from dem all dey earned and made 'em what dey are."

Is she appealing to the government on the ground of economy? When was a democracy ever economical?

Would she have these things happen so that the Negroes could become a strong people?

She has misjudged the psychological formidableness of the white man's feeling of superiority.

The slimness of her audiences worries her. She makes the customary error of berating the individuals who attend her meetings on account of the failure of the absentees to appear.

"You take no interest in de collud pepul. . . . You are de cause of de brutality of these poor creeters. For you're de children of those who enslaved them. Dat's what I want to say.

"I wish dis hall was full to hear me. . . . If Anna Dickinson [a lecturer on Jeanne d'Arc] come to talk here about a woman you know nothing about, and no one knows whether there was such a woman or not—you would fill dis place. You want to hear nonsense. I come to tell you something which you ought to listen to."

For all her exceptional intuition, Sojourner is unable to understand that, now that slavery is no longer an issue, white folk have lost most of their former enthusiasm for the Negro cause. Aged as she is, her body a trifle bent from the numerous campaigns, and her voice a shade huskier than it used to be, she presents a rather pathetic figure, especially considering her earnestness, as she stands on the rostrum pleading a cause which evokes so little enthusiasm.

She pours forth her soul in one final appeal.

"I want you to sign petitions to send to Washington. Dey say there dey will do what de pepul want. De majority rules. If dey want anything good dey git it. If dey want anything not right dey git it too. You send these petitions, and those men in Congress will have something to spout about. I bin to hear 'em; couldn't make nothin' out of what dey said, but if dey talk about de collud pepul, I will know what dey say.

"Send a good man wid de petitions, one dat will not turn de other side out when he gits to Washin'ton. Let de freedmen be emptied out in de West; git 'em land or an outset; teach 'em to read, an' den dey will be somebody."

Even this gigantic task of traveling over the country to stir up interest in her plan cannot completely absorb her amazing energies. She is back in Battle Creek for the presidential election. Respite! She must stump for Grant. She will be a good Republican.

Apparently the Democrats are somewhat averse to her onslaughts against Greeley for, although she attracts an audience so immense that half the throng has to stand and many hundreds are turned away, the Battle Creek *Journal* reports: "The old lady was somewhat 'scattering' in her remarks, but she kept firing away, and occasionally a winged duck went out of the crowd, shrieking."

Will this woman never cease her bold forays into forbidden paths?

Here on the Saturday before election, because she has stumped the country so vigorously for Grant, she demands of the Board of Registration in her home city that her name be entered upon the list of voters! This is the woman who years ago showed her breasts to a mob in Indiana because they said she was not a woman!

Of course the demand is not granted; the idea is unheard of even from these revolutionary exponents of Woman's Rights. Is the old woman deterred? Not a bit. On election day she appears again; this time she insists upon her right to use the ballot. Against the Board's polite refusal she counters arguments filled with all the logic and incision she can command. But to no avail. . . . . Well, at least then, she will have a look at the polls.

"Show me the poll," she requests of a bystander.

When it is pointed out to her, she stares at the place wide-eyed and open-mouthed.

In her mind she had pictured a barber or a telegraph pole!

Drudgery.

Even Sojourner is beginning to doubt. What is the matter with these folk who in other days always rallied so vigorously?

"Everybody," she tells a friend, "tells me to 'stir 'em up.' But I ask you, 'why don't *they* stir 'em up?'—as though an old body like myself could do all the stirring."

The Liberia substitute-proposal vexes her.

"Why should the American Negro go to Liberia? Instead of sending these people to Liberia, why can't they have a colony in the West? This is why I am contending so in my old age. It is to teach the people that this colony can just as well be in this country as in Liberia."

She is becoming exhausted from her efforts.

"Everybody says this is a good work, but nobody helps. How glad I will be if you will take hold and give it a good lift. Please help me with these petitions."

She is in the East once more, and she takes time out to have a fling at modern motherhood.

"Women," she enjoins a group of mothers in Providence, "you forget that you are the mothers of creation. You forget your sons were cut off by the war, and the land was covered with their blood.

"You rig yourselves up in panniers and Grecian-bend backs and flummeries; yes, and mothers and gray-haired grandmothers wear high-heeled shoes and humps on their heads, and put them on their babies, and stuff them out so they keel over when the wind blows.

"Oh, mothers, I'm ashamed of you! What will such lives as you live do for humanity? When I saw these women on the stage at the Woman's Suffrage Convention the other day, I thought—what kind of reformers be you, with goose wings on your heads, as if you were going to fly, and dressed in such ridiculous fashion, talking about reform and women's rights? 'Pears to me, you had better reform yourselves first."

The old Sojourner once more. What would she be saying to-day?

Was this the time that she visited President Grant and got him to sign his name in her book? No doubt. But he was in a "drefful hurry," and could give her no such interview as Lincoln afforded her. This was on March 31, 1871.

A western trip in the latter part of 1871 occasions an amusing newspaper controversy.

The St. Louis *Dispatch* revives the male ghost.

"Sojourner Truth," it reports, "is the name of a man now lecturing in Kansas City. He could only be called a 'sojourner' there, for truth could not abide in that place as a permanent resident."

The Leavenworth *Times*, rushing to Sojourner's rescue, calls the *Dispatch* to account.

"Considerable ignorance is displayed in the first sentence, and an unusual regard for truth in the last."

The Kansas City *Journal* is even more forceful in its resentment of the St. Louis report.

"Ignorance of the sex of the noted personage, Sojourner Truth, by the writer of the above, is proof of wonderful lack of information. Certainly, knowledge does not sojourn in that head, and truth without knowledge has but poor dispatch in the affairs of men and women."

Like John Dumont, these folk certainly find attraction in this doughty warrior!

§ 8

It is now the spring of 1874.

Sojourner is racing about the country, pleading for her plan as if she were fifty years younger than the seventy-six or -seven she can certainly lay claim to. She carries along with her numerous petitions, each one filled with signatures and looking like an exercise sheet in handwriting. She is ready to leave Battle Creek once more, and go to Washington in order to present her signatures to Congress.

Naïve creature! Does she imagine that Congress, which has nearly impeached Johnson on account of these same Negroes, and is now making life a veritable hell for Grant, will move three million Negroes westward simply because she has collected signatures?

Off she goes, however, joined by her favorite grandson, Sammy Banks, who meets her in Ohio, and proceeds with her by gradual stages to the capital.

She reaches Washington, but the sentence of doom is written almost from the day she arrives. Her grandson takes ill with a consuming disease, and she is forced to hurry back to Battle Creek in an effort to save his life. The effort is in vain, alas! for in February, 1875, Sammy Banks passes away.

Now Sojourner is sorely grieved, more sorely grieved, perhaps, than we have ever known her to be.

She was inordinately fond of this grandson. She had carried him around with her since he was a tiny fellow. Harriet Beecher Stowe has told of the great amusement she received from watching his pleasing antics, as a small youngster, when Sojourner made her renowned visit to her home, and of Sojourner Truth's great attachment to the boy. As he grew into manhood, he became a right-hand staff, accompanying her on many of her long travels, and helping her by reading to her the passages of the Bible which were so essential to her mode of expression.

Now he is gone, and the woman is nearly broken-hearted. It is hard to travel about, alone, at eighty years or nearly that, making speeches for a hopeless cause. Still the work must go on! And go on it does. Sojourner continues to travel, fighting not only for her dearest concern, but for Woman's Rights and Temperance as well. But while she will do anything or go anywhere if she thinks she can further the plan to transfer Negroes to Kansas, she much prefers now, when she is able, to remain at home, making occasional speeches at the Battle Creek Health Sanitarium, where she is a favorite among the scores of patients, who purchase her photographs and her biography, thus enabling her to sustain herself.

In reality, however, her physical endurance had reached low tide, and her health was breaking. The fever sores which had brought an end to Mau-Mau-Bett now recurred in Sojourner. Varicose ulcers appeared on her legs, sometimes making bands completely around them to a width of three or more inches.

An amusing, though rather shocking, story is told by the physician who treated her during these illnesses. He was called to attend Sojourner and found her suffering from these ulcers. After giving her proper treatment, he saw no more of her for about six weeks. Then she came to him, this time with a more severe case of varicose sores.

"Why, Aunty Sojourner," her physician asked her, "what have you been doing?"

"Well, doctor," Sojourner replied, "I thought those salves and other medicines you gave me were too mild for anyone as tough as I am, so I went to the horse doctor and he gave me something that was real strong; but I guess it's made it worse!"

The art of skin grafting had recently been discovered. This physician decided to employ it in Sojourner's case. He asked one of Sojourner's daughters to give some of her skin to aid her mother. The poor woman was frightened almost to death, and rushed to a neighbor, imploring her protection against the man who proposed to skin her alive.

Thereupon the physician laid bare his own arm and breast, stripped skin from his own body, cut it into small pieces, and applied it in little islands to Sojourner's legs, bandaging the grafted portions into place. The skin united perfectly with her own flesh, and the operation seemed to be completely successful.

The years are passing swiftly.

Sojourner has resisted the inroads of grief over the loss of her grandson; she has conquered her own bodily ailments; time and time again she has tramped from one part of the country to another, hundreds, yea, thousands of miles, if only she might convert a few scattered souls to her great plan. But the road grows constantly more uphill, while the sands in her hourglass rapidly diminish.

These are the days when Sojourner Truth herself believes that she is a hundred or more years of age. She calculates her birthday from the date of her freedom, which she says is the year 1817, although we are sure it was just prior to 1827. She believes, too, that she was forty years of age in 1817, although we are quite sure that Vale was correct in estimating her years at about thirty-eight in the year 1835.

The clue to this mystery probably rests with an interpretation of the New York statute. It did say that all Negroes forty or over should be freed in 1817, and *all* other Negroes in 1827. As Sojourner got older, she imagined that she had been freed in 1817, in other words, that she was at least forty years of age in 1817. But this is impossible, because we know that she was with Dumont just prior to 1827, as his letter of recommendation written during the Matthias trial clearly states. Had Sojourner been forty years of age in 1817 Dumont would have been required by the law to free her. Besides, we have Dumont's word that she was about twelve in 1810.

There is every reason, therefore, for believing that the testimony of her age in these later days is incorrect.

Myth and actuality are difficult to separate at this point. It is said that at one time during these latter years Sojourner's hair had grown completely white, and her eyesight had almost entirely vanished. She herself added that her right side had been totally paralyzed, including her right eye, and that at one time the fever sores on her limbs developed gangrene so badly that friends fainted at sight of her.

Once during this period the rumor actually got abroad that she had died. This, of course, was false. She did not die, but according to fairly well authenticated evidence not only did she completely regain her health, but with it the color of her hair, and the sight of her eyes—in fact, she was able to discard the spectacles which she had been accustomed to wear for thirty or forty years! Some have even gone so far as to state that new teeth formed in her mouth; but we are quite certain that such new evidences as may have appeared in her dentition were of the manufactured variety.

Nearly ten years have flown, and the dream still is far from fact.

Is Sojourner's last and greatest endeavor to result in complete debacle? After this long life of activity, this life in which she has feared nothing and nobody, in which she has participated in cataclysmic efforts of world significance—is she to pass into the vale an acknowledged failure in her life's greatest single ambition?

Is she to quit this mortal coil, herself believing that her dream is doomed, or will she die imagining that the dream will some day see reality?

None of these things.

She is too filled with faith to yield to cynicism, or even to admit defeat; and she is too intelligent not to perceive facts. Despite the tenacity of this hope which never entirely forsakes her, she begins to realize that there is a common-sense reality about all this business of orienting the Negro, and that no immediate solution of the Negro problem is possible. Instead of being discouraged, she becomes more positive than ever where the future of the Negro is concerned.

Almost in the last year of her life, she prepares to go to Kansas to meet with the vanguard of some of the Negroes who she has dreamed would settle in the West on lands bestowed by the government. She will take to them the old message of courage and hope, and of the potentialities inherent in her colonizing plan; but by this time she envisions something far more significant for America and certainly more fundamentally correct than she dreamed in those days when she first conceived her plan in Washington.

She beholds now, not the vision of a Negro race set apart in American life, working out its salvation alone, so that it may be observed, like a molecule in a test tube, proving itself worthy of a place in civilization; no, not that. She has envisioned something far more realistic, far more majestic, far more ambitious, and infinitely more worthy. That mind of hers, brilliant in youth, seems even more brilliant in these waning days when she takes the time to look back quietly over the lessons she has learned out of the experiences of a long past, and then looks ahead confidently and serenely to the days which are to be.

Listen to this oracle as she breathes the vision which her soul has glimpsed. Expressed in the conventional English of a recorder who originally jotted it down in her own quaint dialect, it represents one of the grand prophecies of modern times.

"I have prayed so long," she says, "that my people would go to Kansas, and that God would make straight the way before them. Yes, indeed, I think it is a good move for them.

"I believe as much in that move as I do in the moving of the children of Egypt going out of Caanan—just as much."

She still clings to her dream. Naturally. But this dream

is about to blossom into a grand promise. Those eyes of hers, filled with that peculiar mystic light, are seeing things which she herself can scarcely appreciate; but like the true seer she expresses even that which she does not understand.

Listen, America.

"It will also be a benefit to the South. . . . The blacks can never be much in the South. . . . But if they come to the North, and get the northern spirit in them, they will prosper, and returning down there, *some of them will teach these poor whites.*" (Had she dreamed of Carver and Herndon?)

Listen, America.

"These colored people will bring the whites out of Egyptian darkness into marvellous light. The white people cannot do it, but these will."

What are you seeing, Sojourner Truth? A true democracy of black and white? Minds and hearts of black folk, joined hand in hand with white folk, guiding America to true freedom?

Are you looking ahead to the great economic upheaval of the twentieth century, with its renewed emphasis on the majesty of toil, its insistence on the rights and the place of the worker, its appeal even to black workers to come to the material and spiritual rescue of America—its crowning realization that the division of the races is fatal to white as well as to black?

Listen, America!

"They will teach the slave-holders the truth that they never had and never knew of. . . . These colored people are going to be *a* people. Do you think God has had them robbed and scourged all the days of their life for nothing!"

Sojourner has envisioned the coming world—a world in which a black skin will be a badge of honor; indisputable proof that its possessor is a peer among those whose work is to construct the only true civilization—the coöperative society. Her body sways slightly to and fro, her head shaking with the emphasis of her remarks. Old Sojourner Truth has risen to the highest point in her career. It is a grand climax. It is a glorious achievement of faith and divination.

This Sojourner Truth *is* a sibyl—an oracle. Call her what you will—crazycat, ignoramus, fool, imbecile—hurl whatever epithets it pleases you to hurl—scorn her for her blackness, and rail at her for her pride—this woman is *God's* fool!

She not only steadfastly believes her God, she *hears* Him. That is the point of her remark to many educated folk: "You read books; God Himself *talks* to me."

She can afford to make a virtue out of the very thing which so many unthinking persons hold against her, namely, her black skin. When Lucretia Mott, broken down from the weight of years, inquires of her, "Sojourner, how is it that I am so wrinkled, while you with more years than mine have a face which is just as smooth as can be?" Sojourner's reply, given in the half-arrogant, half-gleeful manner which is so characteristic of the woman, is, "Well, I have *two* skins. I have a white skin under, and a black one to cover it."

In her mind she is a special child of God . . . . and all her people are His *particular* people.

Sojourner was experiencing the vision of the dying.

For more than a year her health had been failing noticeably. The ulcerous condition of her limbs caused intense suffering. The skilful physician who attended her could assuage her pain, but he could not countermand Time. Sojourner was wearing out. At long last not even her great concern will sustain her.

She had never feared death. Once, when someone had mentioned the subject to her, she said that she compared death to stepping out of one room into another, from darkness into light.

"Oh," she exclaimed, "won't that be glorious!"

Now, a broken woman, her body racked with pain, she speaks calmly and confidently, "When we are done with these old bodies, their aches and pains, we shall be gods."

A friend visited her a few weeks before the end. She had endured a night of extreme pain and suffering, but the presence of her friend caused her face to light up with a smile, and she began to sing the song which was her special favorite—the one she had used to subdue the hoodlums at Northampton:

> It was early in the morning,
> It was early in the morning,
> Just at the break of day,
> When he rose, when he rose, when he rose
> And went to heaven in a cloud.

Did her singing bring back to her the ancient days of power and triumph, when men and women by hundreds and thousands hung on every word she uttered? Now she sang in a low voice, a voice curiously sweet, her face rapt in quiet expectancy, and her eyes more brilliant even than in her vigorous years. These are the eyes whose spirit the American sculptor, William Wetmore Story, tried to incorporate and glorify in his statue "The Libyan Sybil."

Those eyes were her particular treasure. How truly she had spoken back in 1877 when, after her sight had come back with an amazing burst of power, she said, "The Lord put new glasses in the windows of my soul!"

A few days before her death, while she lies upon her couch with eyelids closed, her friend calls out to her with anguished spirit, "Sojourner, can you look at me?"

Sojourner hears, slowly opens her eyes, which seem to be surcharged with belief and prophecy.

Quietly, earnestly, she looks into the face of her friend.

There is peace in her gaze, and great understanding. These quiet-seeing eyes which have fascinated multitudes of people who have looked into them, and have held thousands by their sheer prophetic power, never, no never, comprehended so much of life and death, of truth and reality, as now; never rested with more confident assurance of the ultimate triumph of humanity over inhumanity. Her battle would be won.

With a sense of infinite relief and absolute contentment, Sojourner slowly closed her eyes again. Thus they remained, while her body lay for several days nearly immobile. She never again opened those eyes. They had seen all she wanted them to see. Their work was done.

She knew.—A people, only just beginning to grasp the implications of a new freedom, already were proceeding to enact the stupendous play which those eyes had visioned.

§ 9

Sojourner Truth died in Battle Creek, at three o'clock in the morning, November 26, 1883.

They robed her for the grave in black nun's veiling, with white muslin cap and folded kerchief. A bunch of exquisite flowers was placed in her right hand, and over the casket were floral emblems representing a cross, a sheaf of ripened grain, a crown—and a sickle.

At two o'clock in the afternoon of November 28, the funeral procession started from her home, No. 10 College Street, to the Congregational and Presbyterian Church of Battle Creek, where nearly a thousand people had already assembled inside.

The pallbearers, some of Battle Creek's most noted citizens, placed the casket in the vestibule of the church. Soon a vast throng, composed of all classes and creeds from the city, passed reverently by the open coffin to take a farewell look at the beloved character.

The Rev. Reed Stuart made the funeral oration, and G. B. Stebbins of Detroit, a comrade in antislavery battles, paid special tribute.

A tremendous crowd follows the body of the departed one to the Oak Hill Cemetery.

Friends gather round the open grave in silent little groups. It is hard to believe that the perennial Sojourner has passed on; that the doughty warrior is never to be seen again trotting along the city streets; that her bewitching voice is forever still.

The long line of carriages, the hearse with its somber black plumes, the huge throng—all stand motionless while the last words are intoned by the minister.

The grave is closed amidst autumnal silence. Later a stone will be placed upon it, bearing the celebrated admonition to Douglass, "Is God Dead?"

It has been a perfect fall day.

Far off in the cloudless sky a great round red ball, which casts purple shadows over distant spires, hills, and tree-tops, hesitates for one quivering instant, gives a last loving touch of pale gold, then sinks slowly under the western horizon.

Selected Bibliography

ONE OF THE chief works is Olive Gilbert's *Narrative of Sojourner Truth* (Boston, 1850). This is also included in Mrs. Frances W. Titus' *Narrative of Sojourner Truth and the Book of Life* (Boston, 1875; Battle Creek, Mich., 1884). The later edition contains a valuable appendix which was compiled after the death of Sojourner Truth. G. Vale's *Narrative of Isabella* (New York, 1835—two volumes in one, and sometimes called *Fanaticism, Its Source and Influence, illustrated by the simple narrative of Isabella*) is indispensable for information relative to the Matthias Delusion, as is William L. Stone's *Matthias and His Impostures* (New York, 1835). Ellis H. Roberts' *New York* (New York, 1915) provides valuable descriptions of life in New Amsterdam and New York State during the seventeenth and eighteenth centuries. For conditions in America prior to, during, and after the Civil War, including in some cases references to Sojourner Truth, the following volumes are very illuminating: Albert Bushnell Hart's *The American Nation*, Vol. XVI; *Slavery and Abolition* (New York, 1906); Maria L. Child's *The Freedmen's Book* (Boston, 1865); Mrs. C. E. McKay's *Stories of Hospital and Camp* (Philadelphia, 1876); Mary Clemmer Ames' *Ten Years in Washington* (Hartford, Conn., 1880); John Preston McConnell's *Negroes and Their Treatment in Virginia* (Pulaski, Va., 1910); John W. Cromwell's *The Negro in American History* (Washington, 1914); Benjamin G. Brawley's *A Social History of the American Negro* (New York, 1921); Carter G. Woodson's *The Negro in Our History* (Washington, 1928); Vernon Loggins' *The Negro Author* (New York, 1931); George W. Williams' *History of the Negro Race in America from 1619-1880* (New York, 1883); and James Allen's *The Negro Problem in the United States* (New York, 1936) and *Reconstruction* (New York, 1937).

INDEX

Index